OUR EDUCATIONAL PROBLEM

OUR EDUCATIONAL PROBLEM

BY

HAR DAYAL., M. A.,

WITH AN INTRODUCTION BY

LALA LAJPAT RAI

GYAN

Published by

Gyan Publishing House
5, Ansari Road
Daryaganj, New Delhi-110002
Phone: 011-47034999, 9811692060
E-mail: books@gyanbooks.com

Distribution Network
gyanbooks.com
India, USA, Canada, UK, Australia, France

ISBN: 978-81-212-7967-3 (PB)
First Published, 1922

2nd Impression 2023

Printed at: Gyan Press, Delhi.

OUR EDUCATIONAL PROBLEM
Author: HAR DAYAL

OUR EDUCATIONAL PROBLEM

OUR EDUCATIONAL PROBLEM

BY

HAR DAYAL., M. A.,

WITH AN INTRODUCTION BY·

LALA LAJPAT RAI

PUBLISHED BY

TAGORE & Co., MADRAS

First Published 1922

CONTENTS

INTRODUCTION

The problem of education has been a kind of complex with me. I have given a great deal of time and energy to study it and to solve it in the interest of my country. I have also made several experiments but so far the problem has baffled my wit. Modern life has complicated the problem very much, but for us in India the hetrogenerity of our population, the fact of a foreign Government and the introduction of a foreign culture has still more complicated the question. There is however one aspect of it on which I find my mind very clear, viz. that the present system of education, as followed and enforced by the official universities of India, and by government-aided institutions is calculated to prolong indefinitely, if not perpetuate our political bondage and also to keep us economically inefficient for a long time to come. Even if, and when we get self-government, it will not be easy for us to acquire economic efficiency, except after long experiments and with a huge outlay of money.

In 1908, when Lala Har Dayal wrote these articles for the "Punjabee" I laboured under the belief that some kind of education was better than no education, but my opinions have since undergone a great change and now I feel that while upto a certain point this education did us a certain amount of good, for some years backwards however it has been productive of positive harm. It has helped in the multiplication of intellectual and economic parasites and retarded our progress towards freedom. At no time in my life had I any doubt about the underlying motive of the British Government in their educational policy, but these articles and some others written by the editor of the Modern Review, published in 1908—10 confirmed me in my suspicions. Mr. Gandhi's propaganda and the opportunities that it has afforded me of testing the effects of this education by experience acquired in the present struggle for political liberty, has strengthened me in my original belief. At the present moment, I strongly believe that this system of education is more harmful than useful; that it is emasculating and enervating; that it is denationalizing and degrading; and that the so-called educated man is more effective a hindrance to our progress in political freedom than his uneducated brother.

Mr. Har Dayal's articles are therefore, of great use in enlightening people on the merits of this question. I therefore welcome the reprint of these articles in the form of this booklet, so readily undertaken at my expressed desire by my friend Mr. Rangildas Kapadia of Bombay. The articles have been reprinted without any changes and do not necessarily represent the present opinions of Mr. Har Dayal. In fact we do not know what his present opinions are. The value of these articles lies less in Mr. Har Dayal's opinions and more in the quotations he has given in support of these opinions. I wish the publishers could have added Modern Review articles also, in order to make this volume complete for reference.

THE VALUE OF WESTERN METHODS AND WESTERN CULTURE

Before I close this brief foreword, I want to add a word about the value to us of Western Culture and Western Methods. On that point I have expressed myself fully in my book on "The problem of National Education in India" published by Messrs. George Unwin & Co., London. It would perhaps suffice if I say that in the main I still adhere to the opinions expressed therein. If I were to rewrite the book, I should change it in certain respects, but that change would not materially affect my fundamental beliefs. The West has made great advance in the theory and methods of education. India cannot ignore the scientific knowledge and scientific methods of the West except at her peril. The culture of the West with its horrible abominations, contradictions and cruelties, is not a thing to be disposed. Indians must study and assimilate it if they can. We cannot even avoid and keep out its evil characteristics without mastering it. If, therefore, I am so bitterly opposed to the education enforced and encouraged by the Official Universities of India and by Government-aided or affiliated schools, it is not because I am opposed to Western culture and Western sciences, but because of its inherent tendencies to develop a slave mentality and a slavish character in our boys. This education—I mean the methods and the processes of it—make us despise our own culture and our own language. It breeds in us habits and manners which cannot be satisfied without resort to European goods, and an imitation of European habits of life. But most of all because it makes us economically dependent on crums thrown from the table of a foreign Government and an alien people. It destroys native pride, native self-respect and native self-confidence. It encourages loyalty to a foreign Government, and loyalty to foreign ideals. This was the object which its founders had in view and it has been well fulfilled. The articles of L. Har Dayal leave no manner of doubt in this respect and therein lies their value to the present generation of Indians.

LAJPAT RAI

OUR EDUCATIONAL PROBLEM

IDEALS OF EDUCATION

Education has been defined as a process of training and development that enables individuals or nations to make the best use of the faculties with which they have been endowed. The individual cannot work out his moral, intellectual and physical growth unless he profits by the accumulated experience and wisdom of generations gone by, and the nation is prevented from attaining its full stature and realising its destiny in the scheme of the Universe, if the individuals composing it are denied the opportunity of developing their gifts and capacities according to the most efficient methods known to the age when they happen to be born.

But man cannot live and grow alone. He is a gregarious animal. He is meant to be social and sociable. He who loves solitude, it has been wisely remarked, is either a God or a beast. Human nature is so constituted that men have always found delight and satisfaction in association as a primary condition of their welfare. Isolate a man from his fellow-beings, shut him up in a secluded corner away from the haunts of men, and he will dwindle and decay till all that is best in him, his intellect and impulse, his social instincts, and his moral nature, perishes so utterly that he is reduced to the level of a brute.

Association brings home to a man the duties that he owes to others, and thus supplies the one condition essential to moral development. For him who comes into real contact with all types and ranks of men, human brotherhood remains no empty phrase, but becomes a living creed ennobling and elevating his every day conduct. Thus the first object of education ought to be to impress on the mind of every child the sanctity of his duty to humanity which may be translated into theological language as his duty towards God. As the soul is the immortal part of man, as morality takes precedence of the intellect in all systems of conduct, we must place the gradual evolution of the sense of duty to mankind as the primary object of a healthy educational system. If this result is secured, the race will produce many noble men, whose names are cherished by millions after them ; but if this ethical aspect to education is ignored, the nation will give birth to moral and intellectual pygmies, contemptible creatures whose lives are short, miserable and brutish. Thus does *Dharma* protect a race which keeps it alive, as the ancient *Rishis* declared. But this great *Dharma* of universal charity and goodwill, this ideal of *Ahimsa*, cannot be realised by an individual, unless he first establishes particular relations with the smaller social unit of which he forms a part. A long process of historical evolution has resulted in the formation of well-defined, compact social groups, which are marked off from one another by distinct and unmistakable features relating to manners and customs, language and religion, history and social environment. These groups of men associated together in States, tribes, *Jirgahs* or clans, are called 'nations', and a nation is therefore that a portion of humanity in the midst of which an ordinary man lives, moves and has his being for all practical purposes of life. Before Steam and Electricity caused that shrinkage of the world which enables us to go round the globe in 80 days, these nations remained more or less isolated from one another, each following the path of development on which it had set out in the early portion of its history. The 19th century almost annihilated space, has brought the Briton next door to the Zulu and the Malay, and has lifted the veil from off the face of Tibet. Nothing is now inaccessible to man, except perhaps the South Pole. The doctrine of nationality has thus been brought to prominence as the chief factor in the struggle which has followed the increased opportunities for intercommunication.

God has so willed it that mankind should contribute to the advent of the "far off divine event to which the whole creation moves" by dividing themselves into large groups which possess different capabilities and aptitudes, and are bound together by special ties of blood and religion and common history. Unity in variety seems to be the law of human progress as revealed in the history of the world for the last 3,000 years. A man can fulfil his duty to humanity by trying to come into direct contact with his fellowmen at the antipodes and ministering to their wants, but in that case his life will bear no relation to his actual surroundings. He will waste his energies in running after a phantom, in building a superstructure without a foundation. A mere cosmopolitan may entertain noble aspirations, but he cannot embody his ideas in the present. All the institutions of a race depend for their vitality on a proper relation between the educational system and the facts of external life. A type of character which does not accord with the social environments or the institutions of the nation will be a cause of disintegration and disorganization. Harmony between the individual spirit and the social group which should lead the former to subordinate its selfish promptings to the good of the latter, is essential for national existence.

Having developed the national type of character and brought it into line with the national modes of life, education should direct the youth to activities which should afford him an opportunity of fulfilling his duty to the nation. Hence the choice of a profession, which confronts a man as the gravest of problems at the threshold of life. We regard a profession as the sphere of work in which a man fulfils his *Dharma*. A profession is not meant to enable one to carn a livelihood for one's selfish purposes. We reject without hesitation the individualistic theories of livelihood propounded by those who confound the man with the stomach. The necessity of earning a livelihood is patent. Says Herbert Spencer in his essay on education: "We need not insist on the value of that knowledge which aids in direct self-preservation by facilitating the gaining of a livelihood. This is admitted by all and indeed by the mass perhaps too exclusively regarded as the end of education.

The choice of a profession supplies a man with the material wealth without which national existence is impossible, or it enables him to render services to society which are indispensable for its welfare. Hence all professions in a healthy society may be divided into productive and non-productive: the former category including those callings which directly produce commodities for enjoyment, and the latter class comprising those avocations which do not directly help in the production of commodities, but which preserve the conditions necessary for the production of commodities. Persons who perform functions other than the production and transmission of wealth are allowed a share of the wealth produced by the community not as a personal reward for doing their duty, but as a means of enabling them to discharge that duty in the best possible manner. Hence it is a mistake to regard income and professions from a selfish point of view —everything must be subordinated to *Dharma*.

Hence we find that an ideal system of education should satisfy the following conditions :—

(1) It must awaken in boys a sense of their duty to humanity and the nation ;

(2) It must form the national type of character ;

(3) It must accustom boys to the national modes of life and thought which are around them ;

(4) It must make them fit for some form of activity, by which they should develop their nature and carry out their *Dharma*.

This form of activity is called a Profession and the allowance of material wealth accorded to the person by the Society is called his Income. Thus Livelihood follows tangible institutions without taking help from the living doctrine of Nationality. For it is so ordained that no one, not even a Tolstoy, shall establish direct relations with Humanity except through the transforming medium of National Sentiment. We may in our impatience find fault with this ordering of human events as the product of narrow minds and half-developed moral instincts. We may look upon the principle of nationality as a stumbling block in the way of the man who tries to rise to the full height of his nature. But there it is, the hard fact of life, which one can deny only at his peril—the deep, ineradicable, irresistible instinct that shattered the cunningly woven fabrics reared by the clever hands of a Joseph II and a Napoleon. You may as well deny the presence of family affection as a determining factor in social affairs. Indeed modern history resolves itself only into a record of the assertion by nationalities of their separate consciousness as against the encroachment of some 'Imperial' power.

The education, which aims at making a perfect man of the child who is born to-day, should enable the young boy to realize his duty to Society and Humanity in general ; and for the effective discharge of that obligation it should teach him his responsibilities towards that portion of mankind in whose history and character he naturally participates, and among whom he will live and grow and form close and enduring relations extending to all activities that help to further his individual progress.

Thus is the *Darmah* of *Ahinsa* related to the *Dharma* of national existence as the abstract to the concrete, as the general to the particular, as the ideal to the actual.

Hence the Primary object of my well-devised sound system of education in a civilized country should be the awakening of a sense of duty to the nation as the largest practicable social unit towards which an average man can establish constant relations, and with regard to which he can assume definite responsibilities. What shall it profit a nation if it gain the whole world but lose its own soul, like ancient Rome in the later days of empire, like Ireland in the nineteenth century. Learning, wealth, culture, polished manners, art and science in their most beautiful forms,—all these will follow in due time of this essential requisite of individual and national growth is provided, viz., the Patriotism or *espirit de corps* which inspires those who realise their duty towards the nation.

How is this result to be brought about? What are the methods by which a community keeps alive the vital principle which alone can preserve it from decay? How is this Promethean spark to be kept up in successive generations like the never-to-be-extinguished *Jyoti* that lights up the shrine of Badrinath? For it cannot be asserted too often that a system of education whlch impairs or does not develop a sense of social duty is worse than useless, even though it should turn out intellectual prodigies and cover the face of the land with academies and institutes. Not by science alone does a nation live and thrive. No amount of booklore or scientific knowledge or oratorical gifts, no discoveries in the domain of science or archæology, no laurels placed on the brows of savants by admiring nations, no literatures and philosophies can compensate a nation for the weakening, even in the slightest degree, of that social spirit which constitutes its vitality. How foolish would a people be who sold away their life for little learning? Learning is good, in its place, but the paramount aim of a healthy educational system is the formation and growth of that feeling of social solidarity which is at the basis of all progress.

Education must therefore begin with the history of the race to which the boy belongs. The individuality of a nation consists in the mass of tradition and historical memories which should form the intellectual equipment of even the meanest and the most uncultured member of the social group. This historical tradition distinguishes one nation from another—it is the chief badge of nationality, the sign of freemasonry that gives admission to its sacred circle. All that the race has done is its treasure, the deeds it had wrought, the thoughts it has perfected, the emotions it has felt, the arts it has developed, the revolutions it has undergone, all this and much more the race preserves and transmits from generation as an heirloom never to be cast aside. Thus the boy is made to feel that he is bound by indissoluble ties to those who have gone before him, that he as a part in all the experiences of his race and that he must merge his little life in the vaster and grander life of the nation. The awakening of patriotism through the teaching of national history is thus the *first requisite* of a sound educational system.

And this training resolves itself into several elements :—

(1) The teaching of historical tradition.

(2) The consequent formation of a certain type of character, and

(3) The reproduction of the social environment of the nation in the life of the school, as the customs and manners of a people are the result of the process of historical growth it has passed through.

The formation of the National Type of character and the imparting of a love for the national manners and customs and modes of thought and life follow as corollaries from the duty of teaching of the national historical tradition. The past is brought home to the student as a means of enabling him to do his duty, a profession as a necessary consequence, but is not its main object. A man walking in the sun casts a shadow behind him, but no man walks in the sun for the express purpose of casting the shadow.

We shall in our next discuss the nature of the professions for which a healthy system of education should prepare the boys of a nation, and shall then apply the general principles elaborated above to test the effects of the educational system established in India on the nation's welfare and progress.

CHOICE OF A PROFESSION

The choice of a profession with the object of fulfilling one's social *Dharma* is one of the most important duties in life. In fact nothing moulds a man's character and shapes his course of conduct more effectively than his profession. Some people would regard marriage as a more potent factor in the building up of individual character than profession. But this proposition is not unexceptionable. Let both "divide the crown". Certain it is that a man's wife and his calling exert the greatest influence on him, for better or for worse, throughout his worldly career. It, therefore, behoves us to exercise the utmost care and judgment in the selection of both of them. Let a man consider how he can best benefit his society and choose accordingly. The choice of a profession with the help of advertisements in newspapers is apt to land an honest man in strange difficulties. But how few are those who deliberate about the right or wrong of the vocations which they desire to adopt, who take counsel with themselves as to whether they can conscientiously discharge the duties of the position they intend to take up! Livelihood for its own sake and at any cost seems to be the watchword of "educated" India at present. Bread and butter take precedence of *Dharma*. It is considered a sign of moral puritanism to discuss the moral aspects of any line of conduct that a man may adopt for the purpose of earning his living. This tone of national feeling betrays a sad decadence of the ethical standard of the nation. They who run only after bread shall lose it, but those who follow *Dharma* will obtain both *Artha* and *Karma*, as promised by the sage in Mahabharata. This, then, is the first test which must be applied to any profession—is it socially beneficial? Does it involve no serious breach of the moral law? A profession which raises an able man to the highest pinnacle of fame and glory, but undermines the vitality of the nation, stands self-condemned. I shall discuss the bearing of this great principle on the question of "Government Service", "the Bar" and other cognate topics.

Further, a profession must enable man to do the maximum of good to his nation. It is not enough to persuade oneself that one is not inflicting any injury on humanity in general. It is necessary that every citizen should exert himself with all his might to make himself serviceable to the "State" which represents his community. A profession is one of the many paths to perfection which are open to him, and he should always consider himself responsible to the "State" for the use that he makes of his powers of mind and body. If a man endowed with uncommon intellectual gifts becomes a cobbler or a hawker, he is cheating humanity of its due. He is an unfaithful steward. His profession is only a negative form of theft.

Having indicated the general principles on which we must proceed in order to construct a healthy educational system for our boys, we should apply them to our present day problems. And there lies the rub. Most of the truths outlined above are, people would say, mere truisms. Every school boy knows them, or at least ought to know them. Every president of a University Convocation dins these beautiful formulae into our ears. We are tired of them. Let us hear something new. Mark Twain at Geneva said to the guide who showed him an Egyptian mummy, "Sir, I have not travelled so far to see an old corpse." Even so our "educated" men may turn away in disgust from these old friends who are always reappearing with new faces.

I admit the justice of this complaint. But I desire to vary the theme. I do not wish to indulge in mere platitudes about educational ideas. I wish to apply them to existing conditions, a painful and arduous task. I shall now proceed to show how

(i) the "educational" system established by the

British Government in India is unsound, abnormal and pernicious in all its ramifications.

(ii) a national educational system can be evolved out of the material that at present is at our command.

Let us take up the work of destructive criticism first. The jungle must be cleared before we can make a road through it. The self-complacency of the "educated" classes who are never weary of admiring one another as products of the "University System" must receive a shock before they can realize the aims and effects of English educational policy in India. Old gods must be dethroned. However painful the process may be, it must be done. I feel keenly on this point. *British educational policy is killing out the soul of the nation.* The whole machinery of schools and colleges, 'normal' and 'abnormal', aided and unaided, Vernacular and Anglo-Vernacular, is one huge octopus which *is sucking out the moral life-blood of the nation.* It is crushing out the heart and conscience of our middle and upper classes. Oury oung men are slowly dying a death, far more dreadful than mere physical dissolution, infinitely more pitiable than the end of the crazy suicide—a death of all that is noble and praiseworthy in their character and habits, a social, moral and intellectual death which leads to no resurrection, either in this world or the next. This spectacle of a nation killing its *Self,* its *Life* without knowing it, moves me to tears, Alas that it should be so!

I know there are persons, perfectly "honourable men", who look upon the British educational system as the panacea for our ills. For all purposes of social, political and religious reformation, they prescribe only one formula "Education". But they do not stop to inquire: "What sort of education?" They take it for granted that the educational facilities afforded by the British Government will lead to the progress of our nation. This belief is a sort of religion with them. It is heresy to dispute it. An Anglo-Vernacular High School is to them a temple: a College is *airtha* (holy place of pilgrimage). I shall dispose of their arguments after a discussion of the *objects* and the *effects* of the educational system established by astute and far-seeing foreigners in our country.

THE EDUCATIONAL POLICY OF THE GOVERNMENT

Nothing is more instructive than history. Let us see how and why the British Government established schools and colleges in India after the establishment of their dominion. There are two sides to this question.

Some people would have us believe that the rulers took pity on us. They saw an old and capable nation sunk in "superstition and ignorance." They came as representatives of a progressive civilization glorious in arts and arms. They desired to raise these poor, illiterate Hindus, "half devils, half children", to their own level.

They came as merchants and tax-gatherers; but as time passed they began to think of better things than gold. They wanted to make *prayaschitta* for all the sins of omission and commission committed by the pioneers of empire in Bengal and elsewhere. They therefore looked after our health, our education and our general welfare. Heaven-sent missionaries of culture and enlightenment, they have for more than 150 years laboured to impart European knowledge to a rude and untutored race. The British people deserve our heart-felt thanks for this great boon. The English education is a free gift from the Government to the people. The Government may be, in some respects, as bad as some of its critics make out. It may be cruel, exacting, arbitrary. But no one can deny that it has proved its generosity by "educating" us, thus converting the old-fashioned, uncouth Pandits into wideawake "graduates" who are ever in touch with the latest developments of modern civilization. What a transformation! Alas! had the Gods churned the ocean a little longer, they would surely have found a fifteenth *Ratna* in the shape of "English education". What a pity that Narada was not born in this age of Universities! Let us praise the Government that has made us men. Mr. Mehta has spoken times without number of the "priceless boon of education". Here, at last, after patient search, we have found one "blessing" of British Rule—a real, tangible, positive "blessing", visible to all and sundry. Let us hold it fast. It is our only hope.

Further the advocates of English educational policy contend that the British showed rare magnanimity in thus accepting us as pupils. Western education imparted in their schools will surely lead to our political enfranchisement. The British knew this full well; but they were inspired by a lofty sense of duty. They could not help doing their duty as rulers. It is in their blood. Duty, dominion and drink are their favourities. The early rulers of India realized that education would one day result in the political emancipation of the people. Yet they persevered. What a sight! Here are a body of foreign conquerors who have acquired sovereignty over a large country after a hundred years' hard fighting. Their dead lie unburied by the Kaveri and the Sutlej; their blood has watered many a field of battle. And now they systematically set themselves to undo all their work, to pave the way for self—extinction, by imparting education to the conquered races. Bentinck and Canning laboriously reverse the process initiated by Clive and Warren Hastings. The first Governors-General were of course mere adventurers; they thought only of taxes. But a generation of sympathetic, benevolent and far-sighted statesmen followed: Munro, Elphinstone, Bentinck, Macaulay. They consulted the welfare of the ruled. They established Schools, Courts, Dispensaries, Post Offices. They undertook the work of "consolidation" and "improvement". Blessed be their names. Let them be added to the Hindu pantheon.

They were not blind. Macaulay's famous despatch mentions the possibility of the grant of "European institutions" to Indians as a consequence of education. Lord Ellenborough said to Dwarka Nath Tagore that education meant the end of British autocracy. Mr. Mehta is fond of relating how Elphinstone pointed to a heap of educational text-books and said to Gibbs, "But that is our high-road back to Europe". Such pathetic stories have been related by several politicians. The Anglo-Saxon race is convinced that if Empire and Duty can't go together, the former must be sacrificed. This spirit should entitle the British rulers of India to a heavenly shower of flowers (*pushpa-varsha*), the reward of great virtue in Hindu mythology. Macaulay, Ellenborough and Elphinstone have taken us into their confidence; they have shown us the workings of their innermost soul. Here is unimpeachable evidence.

I hope I have set forth the views of the apologists for English education fairly and impartially. The speeches and writings of popular "leaders" like Mr. Gokhale and others abound in passages extolling the merits of the British educational system and exhorting Indians to praise the Government for its beneficence.

In my next, I shall discuss the real objects of the Government in establishing the educational system in India, basing my remarks on evidence extracted from official or semi-official documents. The confessions of an official are always interesting reading. They may remind us of another book by Colonel Meadows Taylor that we read in our school days. But that is, of course, merely coincidence.

THE REAL OBJECTS OF BRITISH EDUCATIONAL POLICY

The enlightened politicians who teach us that the Government established schools and colleges for our benefit, have perhaps not read the history of India in the nineteenth century. It is a pity that they should spread such erroneous ideas without studying the records which tell of the motives that animated the British conquerors to undertake the difficult task of imparting education to their subjects. General principles of Sociology deduced from a critical study of the history of the world may also help us in gauging the ideas that underlie the educational system of the Government. There is nothing new under the sun. What has been, is and shall be for ever more. The history of India in ancient times being enacted over again on the same soil and also in Africa in the twentieth century. The relations of conquering races to their subjects form a very interesting and important study. History teaches us certain laws of general application which have governed and regulated those relations. It should be our aim to discover these great truths, which are as precious as any spiritual treasures embedded in holy lore and to profit by them in our present condition. What the Upanishads are to the individual soul, History is to the collective organization called a Nation—it is the means of self-realization and emancipation.

The British established schools and colleges in India with the object of strengthening *their* hold over the country, of laying firm the foundation of *their* power, of consolidating *their* dominion so that the risks to which a foreign ruler is always exposed may be reduced to a minimum. Of course, if it is assumed that this result has brought India all good and no evil, then and only then can the educational system be regarded as a source of unalloyed bliss for the Indian people. Then it would be, like mercy, twice blessed—it blesses him that teaches and him that is taught. It would envelop both the rulers and the ruled in a halo of glory as a consequence of participation in a common enterprise which produces only beneficial results.

That the British rulers regarded their educational policy as a great instrument for the consolidation of their power is evident from the anticipations they entertained as to its results. Again and again is the hope expressed by officials who ruled in India in the first half of the 19th. century that British schools would be a bulwark of strength to their Empire. They clearly recognized that the pen must retain what the sword had won. The question addressed by the statue of Lawrence in Lahore to every passer-by, " Will you be governed by the sword or pen ?" is misleading. It conceals the truth that we are governed by both sword and pen.

I now quote a few extracts from various sources to illustrate the feelings with which the Government regarded their educational policy in its early days. Mr. Charles Grant in his book on the education of the Indian people, published in 1792-7, remarked : " In success would lie our safety, not our danger."

We shall take the most rational means to remove inherent great disorders, to attach the Hindu people to ourselves, to ensure the safety of our possessions. to enhance continually their value to us.

(Chapter IV).

Sir C. Trevelyan, a relative of Lord Macaulay's who served the East India Company in various capacities and rose to be Governor of Madras Presidency and Member of the Supreme Council in India, wrote a book " On the Education of the People of India" in 1838. He discussed the question of education from all standpoints and came to the conclusion that a million sterling annually expended on the education of the Indians would " render them at once to our rule and worthy of our alliance." He remarked with profound wisdom :—

In following this course we should be trying no new experiment. The Romans at once civilized the nations of Europe and attached them to their rule by *Romanizing them*, or, in other words, by educating them in the Roman literature and arts and teaching them to emulate their conquerors instead of opposing them. Acquisitions made by superiority in war were consolidated by superiority in the arts of peace and the remembrance of the original violence was lost in that of the benefits which resulted from it. The provincials of Italy, Spain, Africa and Gaul, *having no ambition except to imitate the Romans, and share their privileges with them*, remained to the last faithful subjects of the Empire, and the union was at last dissolved, not by internal revolt, but by the shock of external violence, which involved conquerors and conquered in one common overthrow. *The Indians will, I hope, soon stand in the same position towards us in which we once stood towards the Romans.* Tacitus informs us that it was the policy of Julius Agricola to instruct the sons of leading men among the Britons in the literature and science of Rome, and to give them a taste for the refinements of Roman civilization. We all know how well this plan answered. From being obstinate enemies, the Britons soon became attached and confiding friends; and they made more strenuous efforts to retain the Romans than their ancestors had done to resist their invasion.

We may also take a lesson from the Mohammadans whose conquests have been so extensive and permanent......The Emperor Akbar followed up this policy in India. Arabicised Persian was adopted as the language of his dynasty, and *the direction thereby given to the national sympathies and ideas* greatly contributed to produce that feeling of veneration for the family which has long survived the loss of its power.

The Rev. Alexander Duff, the father of Christian Education in India, published a pamphlet in 1837 offering an " Exposition of the late Governor-General of India's last Act." (viz., the Education Act of 1835). The learned missionary remarked :—

When the Romans conquered a province, they forthwith set themselves to the task of Romanizing it ; that is they strove to create a taste for their own more refined language and literature, and thereby aimed at turning the song and the romance and the history, the thought and the feeling and the fancy, of the subjugated people into Romon channels, *which fed and augmented roman interests*. And has Rome not succeeded?

The Great Akbar established the Persian language as the language of business and polite literature throughout his extensive dominions, and the popular tongue naturally became deeply impregnated with it. The literature and the language of the country thus became identified with the genius of his dynasty, and this has tended more than anything else to produce a kind of intuitive veneration for the family, which has long survived even the destruction of their power, and *this feeling will continue to exist until we substitute the English language* for the Persian, which will dissolve the spell, and direct the ideas and sympathies of the natives towards their present rulers. (p. 27).

Sir Alexander J. Arbuthnot, K.C.S.I., who was for some time a Member of the Supreme Council of India, remarked in the course of the Convocation address he delivered to the students of the Calcutta University in 1880 :—

My conviction is that the more thorough and the more complete the education is which we impart to the people of India, the better fitted they will be to *appreciate the blessings of British rule* and the more they will deprecate any material change in the existing order of things.

Sir Richard Temple, Bart., in his well-known book "India in 1880," says:—

Of late certain symptoms of disloyalty manifested by *some limited sections of certain educated classes*, have caused reflections to be made against the effects of education upon native loyalty. But that disloyalty was traceable to social and traditional circumstances quite apart from educational causes, and *was checked, not fostered or encouraged, by eduction.* There doubtless will be found disloyal individuals among the educated classes as there are among all classes in a country subjected to foreign rule. Nevertheless, *a well-founded assurance may be entertained that those natives who have learned to think through the medium of the language and are imbued with the literature and the philosophy of England, will bear towards the English nation that heartfelt allegiance which men may feel without at all relinquishing their own nationality.*

The same distinguished Anglo-Indian writes in another part of the book :—

The harder questions relate to the effects of education on the conduct of these men, on their trustworthiness and integrity, *their loyalty to the British sovereign, their gratitude to their foreign instructors, their attachment to Western civilization, and their sentiments in regard to the existing order of things. The answers to such questions, if thoughtfully rendered, will be found* as satisfactory as could be fairly anticipated.

It should be noticed that two officials declared after fifty years' experience of the effects of British education, that it was a source of strength to the British connection. The rulers of 1835 hoped and prophesied : the officials of 1880 saw the realization of that hope and the fulfilment of that prophecy.

So much for the general aims of British educational policy. It may be asserted that the British considered it their duty to improve and civilize India by strengthening their rule and Anglicising us in our social life, intellectual pursuits and political attitude. I do not wish to enter upon a discussion of this point at present. I set forth what history teaches. Let every one arrive at his own conclusions.

Let us go a little into *details*. How could the educational system strengthen the foundations of English rule in India? How was it that the civilian found an ally in the schoolmaster? Mr. P. M. Mehta thus describes the relation between a British soldier in the Indian army and a teacher in an Anglo-Vernacular Government school:—

> In India, gentlemen, the soldier is abroad and must be: but *the humble schoolmaster is no less indispensable.* He alone can add stability and permanence to the work of the soldier.
>
> (Speech at Bombay Graduates' Association, April 4, 1893)

Let us examine *the process* by which a B.A., B.T. contributes his share of work towards the consolidation of British authority in India. The whole scheme was as clear as daylight to the founders of the educational system.

First:—The educational system brings Indians into close contact with Englishmen and thus encourages mutual regard and esteem. It weakens the feelings of aversion and contempt with which all conquered nations at first regard their foreign rulers, who are different from them in religion, manners and language. It promotes social intercourse between the rulers and the ruled, and softens racial animosities. It cuts at the root of the instinctive repugnance born of patriotism, with which all races regard their conquerors in the period immediately following the conquest when the sores are not healed and bitter memories separate the two communities like a river of blood. Thus the educational system supplies a point of contrast between the rulers and the ruled. The pupil can not divest himself of all respect for his teacher. The violence of racial hatred and prejudice *on the part of the ruled* is really tempered and allayed by the relations that subsist between the teacher and the taught. The gift of knowledge tends to blunt the edge of resentment felt at the loss of national dignity and self-respect. The process undertaken by the ruling power resembled the task that lay before Jahangir after he had got rid of Shah Jahan how to attach Nur Jahan to himself? We know that Nur Jahan refused even to see her husband's enemy for some time. But patience and policy overcame all obstacles. And the recalcitrant widow became the charming empress in due time. Thus Sir C. Trevelyan wrote in 1838:—

The Arabian or Muhammadan system is based on the exercise of power and the indulgence of passion. The earth is the inheritance of the faithful. The Hindu system, although less fierce and aggressive than the Muhammadan, is still more exclusive: all who are not Hindus are impure outcasts, fit only for the most degraded employments, and of course utterly disqualified for the duties of Government, which are reserved for the military, under the guidance of the priestly caste. *Such is the political tendency of the Arabic and Sanskrit systems of learning. Happily for us, these principles exist in their full force only in books written in different languages and in the minds of a few learned men; and they are very faintly reflected in the feelings and opinions of the body of the people. But what will be thought of that plan of national education which would revive them* and make them popular; would be perpetually reminding the Muhammadans that we are infidel usurpers of some of the fairest realms of the faithful and the Hindus that we are unclean beasts, with whom it is a sin and a shame to have any friendly intercourse. *Our bitterest enemies* could not desire more than that we should propagate *systems of learning which excite the strongest feelings of human nature* against ourselves.

Thus Sir C. Trevelyan pointed out in 1838 that the Arabic and Sanskrit educational systems then in vogue in India encouraged national exclusiveness and racial hatred. He went on to say:—

The spirit of English literature, on the other hand, cannot but be *favourable to the English connection.* Familiarly acquainted with us by means of our literature, *the Indian youth almost cease to* regard us as foreigners........., From violent opponents or sullen conformists, they are converted into zealous and intelligent co-operators with us.

Referring to "the young men brought up at our seminaries," Sir C. Trevelyan says:—

Instead of regarding us with dislike, they court our society, and look upon us as their natural protectors and benefactors: *the summit of their ambition is to resemble us.*

Thus British schools and colleges were actually expected to work a miracle, to convert the sons of those who had fought the English in battle into apt and docile pupils who should regard their Christian rulers as their guides and Gurus. What a change!

Lord Ripon in 1882 said:—

That object is, in the main, to *bring together and unite the European and the native* in the common pursuit and the common love of knowledge.

Lord Mayo hinted at the effect of the educational

system in overcoming the feelings of repugnance which naturally prevented the Indians from mixing with Europeans :—

> I am not without hope that perhaps in the establishment of the school, the college and the University, we may be weaving *a golden band which may bind in closer union the subjects of our Queen*, be they dark or fair, whether they reside in the East or the West." (Address at Calcutta in 1869).

The British rulers realized that, in establishing a common platform on which European and Indian could meet and shake hands, they were strengthening their position in the country. They were drawing the coy Hindu maiden out of the safe zenana of national social exclusiveness in which she had concealed herself away from the sight of unruly admirers.

Thus Sir William W. Hunter, in his book on "The Indian Mussalmans" (published in 1871), enunciated a general principle in these words: "*The chronic peril which environs British Power in India is the gap between the Rulers and the Ruled.*"

Let us ponder over the profound wisdom of this proposition and understand how the educational system helps *British* influence by bridging the gulf between white and brown, and breaking down the barriers, which Hindu exclusiveness had erected between aggressive conquerors of various races and creeds and the weak, divided and spiritless Hindu community.

THE PROCESS OF ASSIMILATION

Secondly:—The consolidation of British rule in India could also be helped by alienating the people, or at least the intelligent and wealthy classes among them, from their national habits and manners, language and literature and then "improving" and "civilizing" them by teaching them to follow the example of their conquerors. This process of Anglicisation could be initiated through the agency of schools and colleges which should instil the new ideas and tastes into the minds of the young men of the nation. This purpose is distinctly avowed by Macaulay in his famous Minute of 1835 about which Mr. C. H. Cameron, President of the Calcutta Council of Education, declared that it "may be considered as the immediate cause of the resolution of Government which settled this great question." This Minute on Education—a document which no thinking patriot can refer to in terms of praise or appreciation—contains sentiments like the following :—

> I doubt whether the Sanskrit literature be as valuable as that of our Saxon and Norman progenitors.

"The question now before us is simply whether, when it is in our power to teach this language (*viz.* Engiish), we shall teach languages (viz. Sanskrit and Arabic) in which, by universal confession, there are *no books on any subjects* which *deserve to be compared to our own*".

"That literature" (i. e. Sanskrit) inculcates the most serious errors on the most important subjects."

"Books which are of less value than the paper on which they are printed while it was blank" (i. e. Sanskrit books).

These extracts illustrate the spirit in which one of the chief founders of the British educational system set about his work. He declared, plainly and unequivocally :—

We must at present do our best to form a class who may be interpreters between us and the millions we govern ; *a class of persons Indian in blood and colour but English in taste, in opinion, in morals and in intellect.*

He confidently looked forward to the day when Britain would have established "the imperishable empire of our arts and our morals, our literature and our laws," in India. This "imperial" sentiment closes the well-known passage which is often quoted with delight by many politicians and in which he admits the possibility of the establishment of "European institutions" in India after some time. The Right Hon'ble Charles Grant, in his treatise published in 1792-7, remarked :—

"Certainly in a political view the great question which this country has to determine respecting India is 'What are the best means of perpetuating our empire there ?'

"At present we are every way different from the people whom we hold in subjection : different in country, in language, in manners, in customs, in sentiments and in religion : their interests also......

they must conceive to be different from ours. What, then, can be a healing principle with regard to all these points, but a principle of *assimilation, a common bond*" (the italics are original) " which shall give to both parties the reality and the conviction of mutual benefit from the connection. Without a uniting principle, a conjoining tie of this nature, we can suppose the couutry to be, in fact, retained only by mere power, but in the same degree that *an identity of sentiments and principles* would be established, we should see a sight new in the region of Hindustan, *a people actively attached, cordially affected to their Government and thus augmenting* its strength."

Mr. Grant then quotes Dr. Robertson to show how Alexander " early perceived, that to render his authority secure and permanent", he must Hellenise his Asiatic subjects, who should " become one people" with Europeans " by obeying the same laws and by adopting the same manners, institutions and discipline." Mr. Grant adds: " It is the leading idea only of this policy, that is meant to be applied here: and that leading idea is plainly the principle of *assimilation*".

Mr. Grant does not wish that the " distinctions between the two races" (in India) " should be lost." He only desires " to attach our subjects by affection, *by interest, by winning them to our religion, and our sentiments*. That would have the effect of rendering our authority permanent and secure."

Evidently Mr. Grant proposed that we should not become completely English in all respects but should cease to be Hindus, thus losing the privileges of both civilizations. He wanted to turn out hybrid outcastes.

Sir Charles Trevelyan wrote in 1838 :—

" Educated in the same way, interested in the same objects, engaged in the same pursuits with ourselves, *they become more English than Hindus*, just as the Roman provincials became more Romans than Gauls or Italians. What is it that makes us what we are, except living and conversing with English people and imbibing English thoughts and habits of mind. They do so too ; they daily converse with the best and wisest Englishmen through the medium of their works, and form perhaps a higher idea of our nation than if their intercourse with it were of a more personal kind ."

The founders of the British educational system in India ardently desired the triumph of the English language all over the world. Sir Charles Trevelyan thus summed up the views of the advocates of English education in 1838 on this point :—

" With a partial exception in Canada, English is the language of the continent of America, North of Mexico. . . . . . . In the West India Islands, we have given our language to a population collected from various parts of Africa. . . . . . Their literature will be the literature of England. More recently the English language has taken root in the continent of Africa itself and a nation is being formed by means of it in the extensive territory belonging to the Cape. But *the scene of its greatest triumphs will be in Asia*. To the South a new continent is being peopled with the English race ; to the North an ancient people who have always taken the lead in the progress of religion and science in the East have adopted the English language as their language of education. . . . . . . The English language, not many generations hence, will be spoken by millions in all the four quarters of the globe, and *our learning, our morals, our principles of constitutional liberty, and our religion, embodied in the established literature and diffused through the genius of the vernacular languages, will spread far and wide among the nations.*"

Professor H. H. Wilson, the famous scholar,

wrote a letter to a journal in 1836, in which he said :—

"I have noticed for some time past repeated effusions in the Calcutta newspapers, advocating a departure from principles hitherto considered sound and just, and *recommending the exclusive* encouragement of English as the first stage of a very feasible project for the annihilation of all the languages of India, vernacular or classical, and the universal use of our native tongue throughout the East. As long as the reveries were confined to the columns of a newspaper they were inoffensive or even amusing ; they assumed more importance when, *in order to prepare for the extermination* of the languages, the suppression of the alphabets was seriously undertaken and Oriental works were printed in characters which the natives could not read."

The hope was also expressed that the social life of the Indians would be transformed. Thus the Right Hon'ble Mr. C. Grant said :—

"Let them acquire a relish for the ingenious exertions of the human mind in Europe, for the beauties and refinements endlessly diversified, of European art and science."

Mr. Grant also spoke of the time when the "English manners, tastes and wants must also have become common."

Mr. Charles Hay Cameron was President of the Council of Education in Calcutta in 1845. The Council, under his guidance, prepared a plan for a University at Calcutta about which, among other things, it remarked :—

"It would encourage the cultivation of the arts and sciences, and call into existence a class of native architects, engineers, surveyors and educated land-holders whose influence would rapidly and certainly diffuse *a taste for the more refined and intellectual pleasures and pursuits of the West.*"

Finally, as regards religion, which is the greatest social force in existence, which provides the sanction for almost every rule of conduct and supports the permanent institutions of society in all countries, Elphinstone, the first English Governor of Bombay, expressed his ideas in these memorable words :—

"To the mixture of religion, even in the slightest degree, with our plans of education, I must strongly object. I am convinced that the conversion of the natives must infallibly result from the diffusion of knowledge among them. Evidently they are not aware of the connexion, or all attacks on their ignorance would be as vigorously resisted as if they were on their religion. The only effect of introducing Christianity into our schools would be to sound the alarm and to warn the Brahmans of the approaching danger."

It is about Elphinstone that the pathetic story is related how he told Gibbs that the education of Indians "was our high road back to Europe."

Mr. Charles Grant's allusions to religion have been quoted above. He also remarked, in another part of his treatise :—

"It might be too sanguine to form into a wish *an idea most* pleasing and desirable in itself, that our religion and our knowledge might be diffused over other dark portions of the globe where Nature has been more kind than human institutions. This is the noblest species of conquest."

The Report of the Committee of Public Institution, dated December 1831, noted with satisfaction that :—

"The encouragement of the Vidyalaya or Hindu College of Calcutta has always been one of the chief objects of the Committee's attention. *The consequence has surpassed expectation.*

A command of the English language and a familiarity with its literature and science have been acquired to an extent rarely equalled by any schools in Europe. *The moral effect has been equally remarkable; an impatience of the restrictions of Hinduism and a disregard of its ceremonies are openly avowed by many young men* of respectable birth and talents and entertained by many more who outwardly conform to the practices of of their countrymen."

Thus we find that a Committee appointed by Government and consisting of responsible officials delights in the notion that the Hindu youths manifest an aversion to their ancestral faith and its sacraments. Elphinstone, in a Minute, dated 13th. December, 1823, has pointed out a possible danger to British rule from the religions of India:—

"In the meantime *the dangers to which we are exposed* from the sensitive character of the religion of the natives and the slippery foundation of our Government. owing to the total separation between us and our subjects, require the adoption of some measures to counteract them; and the only one is to remove their prejudices and to communicate *our own principles and opinions* by the diffusion of a national education."

Sir Charles Trevelyan, in his deposition before a Select Committee of the House of Lords, on the 28th. June, 1853, said:—

"The Bible is not admitted as a class book into Government seminaries. This rule has been objected to, as implying hostility to the progress of Christianity; but no opinion was ever more mistaken. *When we formed English libraries in connection with the different Government institutions, on the re-organization of the system of instruction, after the resolution of 1835, the Bible was placed in all the libraries, and I understand that it is now desired that Mant's and other commentaries on the Bible should also be placed there, thereto I see no objection*..........If we look at actual results, it will be found that of the well-educated converts to Christianity, nearly as many have come from the Hindu College and other Government institutions as from Missionary seminaries. Our text-books on moral philosophy are wholly Christian in their spirit and tendency. In Abercrombie's "Intellectual Powers," which is carefully studied without curtailment, there is a distinct chapter on the evidences of Christianity."

Sir Frederick Halliday, an eminent Bengal Civilian, who was Secretary to the Government of India and afterwards became Lieutenant-Governor of Bengal, gave evidence before a Select Committee of the House of Commons in 1853. In reply to the question whether the Bible should be introduced as a class-book in the Government schools, he said :—

"If anybody says......that the Bible is 'systematically prescribed' or 'authoritatively prescribed,' I cannot understand the meaning of it; persons who write in that way must mean something which I am unable to fathom or they are not acquainted with the facts. *It is not true that the Bible is prescribed in the Government schools; it is put into the Government school libraries universally*, and the students are allowed, to the top of their bent, to read it from beginning to end.........It has been truly said by Sir Charles Trevelyan, in the Committee of the House of Lords, that we are not conscious ourselves to the full extent of the amount of Christian teaching involved in a thoroughly classical English education, independently of all direct efforts at conversion. *It renders necessary a knowledge of the Bible and I may say a knowledge of the great doctrines of Christianity...... I believe there is more knowledge of the Bible in the Hindu College of Calcutta than there is in any Public School in England.*"

Sir W. W. Hunter, Director-General of Statistics to the Government of India, remarked in 1872:—

"No young man, whether Hindu or Muhammadan, passes

through our Anglo-Indian Schools without learning to disbelieve the faith of his fathers. The luxuriant religions of Asia shrivel into dry sticks when brought into contact with the icy realities of Western Science."

He also proposed that, as a remedy for Muhammadan disaffection and fanaticism, a system of Anglo-Arabic schools should be established by the Government. He thus described its advantages :—

" We should thus at length have the Mnhammadan youth educated upon our own plan. Without interfering in any way with their religion, and in the very process of enabling them to learn their religious duties, we should render that religion perhaps less sincere, but certainly less fanatical. *The rising generation would tread the steps which have conducted the Hindus, not long ago, the most bigoted nation on earth, into their present state of easy tolerance.* Such a tolerance implies a less earnest belief than their fathers had. . . . I do not permit myself here to touch upon the means by which, *through a state of indifference, the Hindus and Musalmans alike may yet reach a higher level of belief. But I firmly believe that that day will come and that our system of education, which has hitherto produced only negative virtues, is the first stage towards it.* ("The Indian Musalmans" : p. 214).

In the above extracts, the italics are mine, except where the contrary is indicated.

It is clear that the educational system was expected and intended to produce a revolution in all our institutions, our language, our customs and manners, and our religion, and thus to produce a large and growing *"class of persons, Indian in blood and colour, but English in taste, in opinions, in morals and in intellect."* (Macaulay's Famous Minutes, 1835).

THE CONTROL OF PUBLIC OPINION

The process of "*Assimilation*" to a foreign race, which is popularly known as "denationalization", continues to work. In the meantime, the Government has to look to its safety and stability. A foreign Government must try all means in its power to prolong its existence. It is exposed to so many dangers from all sides that it has been often compared to a settlement on the edge of a volcano. Hence the Government must influence the thoughts of the people according to its conception of what is good and proper. *Ideas* rule in the world. "A thinking man," said Carlyle, "is the worst enemy of the Devil." The mind of the nation cannot be left to itself. Laws and Regulations are passed in order to ensure physical order and peace. But the Mind submits to no Arms Act. It is above coercion. No Government can forcibly compel a man to *think* in a particular manner. The body can be restrained or controlled by power; but who shall forge a fetter for the National Mind and Spirit?

And yet it is clear that unless a Government can control and guide the Thoughts and Opinions of its subjects, it cannot be said to have provided for its security. It may order the newest guns and build the most massive forts but its work is incomplete till it has brought under subjection that which is more powerful than all the armies of the world put together—the Mind and Will of a nation which has not lost its vitality.

The educational system provided the Government with a potent means of guiding and moulding the opinions and activities of our young men. It really served to crush our national "aspirations" and divert our energies into various channels approved by authorities. The necessity of destroying the ideas of national dignity and freedom was patent to the officials who ruled India immediately after the fall of the old dynasties. Thus Sir Charles Trevelyan remarked in his book on Education published in 1838;—

"These views were not worked out by reflection, but were forced on me by actual observation and experience. I passed some years in parts of India, where owing to the comparative novelty of our rule and *to the absence of any attempt to alter the current of native feeling, the national habits of thinking remained unchanged. There, high and low, rich and poor, had only one idea of improving their political condition.* The upper classes lived upon the prospect of regaining their former pre-eminence; and the lower, upon having the avenues to wealth and distinction reopened to them by the re-establishment of a native governmoent. Even sensible and comparatively well-affected natives had no notion that there was any remedy for the existing depressed state of their nation except the sudden and absolute expulsion of the English. After that I resided for some years in Bengal, and there I found *quite another set cf ideas prevalent among the educated natives.* Instead of cutting the throats of the English, they were aspiring to sit with them on the grand jury or on the bench of a Magistrate. Instead of speculating on Punjab or Nepalese politics they were discussing the advantages of printing, and free discussion in oratorical English speeches at debating societies which they had established among themselves."

So we find that the British Schools and colleges were founded to wean our "uneducated" ancestors of the early 19th century from the pernicious habit of "speculating on Panjab or Nepalese politics" and to suggest to them ways and methods of progress more peaceful and "civilized" than the "sudden and absolute expulsion of the English". They were to dispel that perverse ignorance, on account of which the people had "only one idea of improving their political condition." Why could they not form societies for the protection of children and associations for the dissemination of correct knowledge about lice and worms as a preliminary to national regeneration? Poor folk, they were not "educated", and so possessed only one great national "aspiration", the longing for freedom.

Sir Charles Trevelyan pointed out that it was necessary to guide the patriotic and public spirited people among Indians along right lines lest they should stray into undesirable paths. Even our patriotism was to be made to subserve the purposes of Anglo-Indian officials, who were, of course, our "well-wishers." Let our youngmen reflect on the following:—

"There is a principle in human nature which impels all mankind to aim at improving their condition: every individual has his plan of happiness: every community has its ideas of securing the national honour and prosperity. This powerful and universal principle, in some shape or other, is in a state of constant activity; and if it *be not enlisted on our side, it must be arrayed against us. As long as the natives are left to brood over their former independence*, their sole specific for improving their condition is the immediate and total expulsion of the English. *A native patriot of the old school has no notion of anything beyond this: his attention has never been called to any other mode of restoring the dignity and prosperity of his country*. It is only by the infusion of European ideas that *a new direction can be given to to the nationel views*. The young men brought up at our seminaries, turn with contempt from the barbarous despotisms under which their ancestors groaned...... Instead of regarding us with dislike, they court our society......So far from having the idea of driving the English into the sea uppermost in their minds they have no notion of any improvement but such as rivets their connection with the English and makes them dependent on English protection and instruction." (Sir C. Trevelyan in 1838).

Sir Charles was of the opinion that if the English "set the natives on a process of European improvement," the results would be most gratifying to the rulers.

"They will then cease to desire and aim at independence on the old Indian footing. A sudden change will then be impossible; and *a long continuance of our present connection with India will ever be assured to us. A Mahratta or a Muhammadan despotism might be re-established in a month;* but a century would scarcely suffice to prepare the people for self-government on the European model. The natives will not rise against us...... The national activity will be fully and *harmlessly* employed in acquiring and diffusing European knowledge and in naturalising European institutions. The educated classes, knowing that the elevation of their country *on these principles* can only be worked out under protection will naturally cling to us. They even now do so. There is no class of our subjects to whom we are so thoroughly necessary as those *whose opinions have been cast in the English mould.*"

Thus we see that while the old uneducated men of seventy years ago did not know any plan of "restoring the dignity and prosperity" of the nation which did not involve the expulsion of the English from India, the efforts of the Government to give "a new direction" to the "national views" resulted in the production of a class of men who were poles asunder from their fathers, as they could not hit upon any scheme of national improvement which did not make them "dependent on English protection." What a revolution in the public opinion of the country was brought about by the simple process of gathering our young men in classes and suggesting to them new lines of thought and action which lead them away from the political ambitions and aspirations of their fathers! Thus did Government mould the Indian mind immediately after the establishment of the British dominion. At a time when, according to high official authority, "a Mahratta or Muhammadan despotism might be re-established in a month", it was essential for the consolidation of the empire that the national intellect should be brought under proper control, lest we should "brood over our former independence"—a most objectionable and unpatriotic pastime from all stand-points, and particularly so in the eyes of the officials! Sir Charles Trevelyan's words should open the eyes of those who fancy that a denationalising and demoralising educational system has produced, for the first time in the history of India, a "national awakening" which makes men think of freedom. It has had exactly the opposite effect, as is clear from the unimpeachable historical testimony quoted above. Alas the puppets should be unconscious of the presence of the wire-puller!

Charles Hay Cameron, Member of the Council of India and President of the Council of Education for Bengal, published "An Address to Parliament on the Duties of Great Britain to India in 1853." He urged the establishment of Universities in the country and remarked he should "endeavour to frame to himself a distinct notion of *the social and political condition into which it should be our object to bring our Indian empire* by the combind forces of legislation and public instruction." Thus the schools and colleges were to be the instruments for the dissemination of particular ideas of "progress" and "reform among our people". He recommended "an imperial scheme of education" for India.

Sir Charles Trevelyan had clear ideas as to

what was required for the army, which he called "the pillar of our Indian Empire." He was of the opinion that the educational system was à means of promoting loyalty to the British among the military classes.

"The instruction given to the labouring classes can never be more than merely elementary. They have not leisure for more. But, such as it is, they will be indebted for it to us; and as it will form part of a system established and superintended by ourselves, *we shall take care that it is of a kind calculated to inspire feelings of attachment to the British connection.* After this, the young men who enlist in the army will become imbued with the military spirit and moulded by the habits of military obedience. I leave to others to judge whether this training is calculated to make better and more attached, or worse and more disaffected, soldiers than the state of entire neglect, as regards their moral and intellectual improvement, in which the whole class are at present left." (The italics are mine.)

THE ASSOCIATION OF INDIANS IN THE ADMINISTRATION

The safety of every foreign government requires that the rulers should try to associate the intelligent and the influential section of the conquered nation with themselves in the work of "government". No foreign government which desires to provide for its stability, can afford to ignore the wealthy and the cultured classes among the subject people, for it is men of good birth and education who can guide their countrymen and lead them to glory or to ruin as they choose. The leaders of the people must be propitiated; they should be persuaded to identify themselves with the new regime. Unless they definitely throw in their lot with the conquerors, they will be the rallying points for all malcontents who wish to restore the old state of affairs. Their association with the ruling race serves to curb the spirit of the masses and deprives the opposition of its most valuable allies, the natural leaders of the nation.

Hence the foreign government always tries to give the aristocracy of the conquered country some share in the administration of the new State in order to make them and others forget the old times which they had seen, This policy of conciliation is eminently suited to serve the interests of the rulers, for *conciliation and consolidation go hand in hand.* Large empires are generally based on the passive acquiescence of the common people combined with the active and interested support of the influential classes among the conquered races. How to secure the latter requisite of stength and security is the great problem that confronts every Empire builder. So it was with Rome. So it was with Akbar. So it was with the conquerors of India in the early days of the 19th. century. History repeats itself.

The association of the subject people in the administration also gives the ruling race the opportunity of acquiring *social superiority over the conquered races.* Victory in battle confers only military and political supremacy on the rulers. But the acceptance of offices in the administration by important members of the ruled races places within the reach of the new-comers the boon which they ardently long for, viz., a definite place in the social system of the country. They do not desire to occupy a position of social inferiority; they would not sit below the salt. The only method by which they can supplement their merely military occupation with the acquisition and assertion of social superiority in every day life is the association of rich and learned "natives" with the foreign Government, i.e. the bestowal of posts *under* the Executive Head of the alien Administration on proud and patriotic nobles and scholars.

The Court of Directors of the East India Company, in a despatch to the Government of Madras dated 29th. September 1830, wrote:—

> "You are, moreover, acquainted with our *anxious desire to have at our disposal a body of natives*, qualified, by their habits and acquirements, to take a larger share and occupy higher situations in the Civil Administration of their country than hitherto been the practice under our Indian Governments."

The Court of Directors, in a Despatch to the Governor-General in Council of Bengal, declared:—

> "In the meantime we wish you to be fully assured, not only of our anxiety that the judicial offices to which natives are at present eligible should be properly filled, but of *our earnest wish and hope* to see them qualified for situations of higher importance and trust. *There is no point of view in which we look with greater interest at the exertions you are now making for the instruction of the natives than as being calculated to raise up a class of persons, qualified, from their intelligence and morality, for high employments in the Civil Administration of India.* As the means of bringing about this most desirable object, we rely chiefly on their becoming, through a familiarity with European literature and Science, imbued with the ideas and feelings of civilized Europe, on the general cultivation of their understandings and specifically on their instruction in the principles of morals and general jurisprudence. We wish you to consider this as *our deliberate view of the scope and end to which all our endeavours with respect to the education* of natives should refer."

The despatch of the Court of Directors to the

Government of Bombay, dated 29th. September, 1830, contained the following :—

"It is *our anxious desire* to afford to the *higher classes of the natives* of India the means of instruction in European science and of access to the literature of civilized Europe. The character which may be given to the classes possessed of leisure and natural influence ultimately determines that of the whole people. *We are sensible, moreover, that it is our duty to afford the best equivalent in our power to these classes, for the advantages of which the introduction of our Government has* deprived them ; and for this and other reasons of which you are well aware, we are extremely desirous that their education should be such as to qualify them for higher situations in the Civil Government of India, than any to which natives have hither-to been eligible."

Sir John Malcolm, Governor of Bombay, wrote a Minute in 1828 on the question of Education in India. He said :—

"*One of the chief objects*, I expect, of diffusing education among the natives of India, is *our increased power of associating them in every part of our administration. This I deem essential* on grounds of economy, of improvement, and of security.

I cannot look for education of expense in the different branches of our Government from any diminution of the salaries now enjoyed by European public servants, but I look to it from many of the duties they now have to perform being executed by natives on diminished salaries."

A Despatch of the Court of Directors of 1827 urged "the importance of raising up educated natives of high moral character for the discharge of public duties", and added with remarkable candour :—"To this, *the last and highest object of education*, we expect that a large share of your attention will be applied."

So it is discovered that the "highest object of education" is the creation of a class of "native" servants for a Foreign Government! We recommend this grand ideal to those educationists who hanker after University degrees.

Section 72 of the Famous Despatch of 1854, which some politicians, who are fond of dealing in "Charters" for subject races, call "The Educational Charter" of India, explicitly establishes a close connexion between the educational system and the "public" services:—

> "We have always been of opinion that the spread of education in India will produce a greater efficiency in all branches of administration, by enabling you to obtain the services of intelligent and trustworthy persons in every department of Government, and on the other hand, we believe that the numerous vacancies of different kinds which have constantly to be filled up may afford a great stimulus to education."

Section 73 of the same Despatch indicates the desire of Government to obtain efficient servants in larger numbers:—

> "We understand that it is often not so much the want of Government employment, as the want of properly qualified persons to be employed to Government, which is felt at the present time in many parts of India."

The Government not only desired to give offices to the aristocracy, lest Satan might 'find mischief for the idle hands to do', but it also intended to secure a supply of inferior officials at a cheap rate. A tropical country governed by Europeans cannot afford to employ Europeans who demand large salaries before they can undertake a life of royal exile. Hence it is expedient, as Sir John Malcolm recommended, to utilize the services of Indian clerks and daftries, who work for the Government on a mere pittance. All the dirty drudgery of the State offices is to be borne by them. The magnificent fabric of the Empire is to rest on the labours of "sweated" middle-class literate Indians. This class should be made as cheap for Government as possible.

> "From English schools being established at no place but Bombay, the pay of writers and accountants is immoderately high, and when these move from the presidency they require still higher wages; and when well-qualified, they can from their limited numbers, command almost any pay they demand. This introduces a tone of extravagance of demand from this class of persons in all our departments. Of some remedies of this evil, I shall speak hereafter; but *the real mode to decrease price is to multiply the article*. English schools should be established or encouraged at Surat and Poona."
>
> ((Minute by Sir J. Malcolm, Governor of Bombay, 1829)

The employment of the upper classes in the administration is recommended with a view to *conciliate* and *compensate* them, while the association of the middle classes in the work of "government" serves a different purpose. It enables Government to use their powers of mind and body for its own benefit with as little expense to itself as possible. A system of sweating at the bottom surmounted by a system of conciliation at the top, constitutes the essence of the policy of "associating the natives in the administration". The policy of conciliation is also described by some acute and malevolent critics as a policy of Bribery and Demoralization. But what's in a name so long as we understand the truth ?

(c) *The creation of a " dependent class is one of the main objects of the eductional system.* A foreign Government must find some basis of support *within the conquered community,* otherwise it will be short-lived. Its tenure of power will be precarious indeed, if it cannot succeed in inducing some classes among the subject people to identify their interests with the ruling caste. A large number of people, who depend for their rank and subsistence on the favour of any Government, are in duty bound to support it at all times. Their conduct will always be controlled by self-interest. A partition wall of Bread and Butter will divide them from their countrymen. There can be no such class of persons in a country at the time when it is conquered. The new rulers are complete strangers to the people. In course of time they manage to raise a servile caste from among the people, a caste which knows no law higher than the fiat of its employers, no duty more sacred than obedience to the powers that be. It attaches itself to the foreign Government as a dog follows its master for meat. It consents to justify and " interpret" all actions of the Government for the benefit of its subjects. It serves as the medium through which Government can carry out schemes with which it does not wish to associate itself openly. It is the tool of the conqueror, an obliging, supple, unscrupulous, astute, avaricious and hypocritical caste of "Government Servants", devoid of principle, of self-respect, of patriotism. It may be recognized as a caste composed of cruel, cowardly, cunning, cringing, covetous and characterless persons. It is distinguished from other classes as being pre-eminently the characterless caste. This is its great characteristic. The production of such a caste within the social system of the Hindus was, in the words of the Court of Directors, the "last and highest object" of the educational system established by the East India Company. C. H. Cameron, President of the Council of Education in Bengal, said in 1853:—

"The class that we are creating, as we approach towards this great object,—the class imbued with European letters—will be for many generations wholly dependent upon us, much more so than any of the separate and antagonistic classes which we found already extinguished; and they will exceed all those other classes in their enlightened perception of their true position, still more than in the degree of dependence which characterizes it."

THE EXPANSION OF BRITISH COMMERCE

The advocates of the English Educational system in the early years of the nineteenth centuary also looked forward to an increase in the Indian demand for European goods as a consequence of the spread of education in India. Thus the commercial instincts of the ruling race enabled it to realise that the system might "improve" the "natives", but it would certainly enrich the Europeans. Mr. Charles Grant, in his treatise on Indian Education written in 1792-7, said :—" In every progressive step of this work, we shall also serve the original design with which we visited India, that design still so important to this country the extension of our commerce. Let them acquire relish for the ingenious exertions of the human mind in Europe for the beauties and refinements, endlessly diversified, of European art and science, and we shall hence obtain for ourselves the supply of four-and-twenty millions of distant subjects. How greatly will our country be thus aided in rising still superior to all her difficulties, and how stable as well as unrivalled may we hope our commerce will be . . . Wherever we may venture to say, our principle and language are introduced, our commerce will follow."

We have described the objects of British "educational" policy in order that our countrymen may obtain an insight into the principles which the British Government has followed in rearing the magnificent system of Universities, Colleges and schools of various descriptions, before which some of us stand speechless with admiration and gratitude.

History teaches us that all conquering races attempt a social and intellectual conquest of subject races after they have secured political dominion over them. The political conquest only destroys the organized physical strength of a weak nation. But the process of social and intellectual subjugation corrupts and poisons its national life at its very source. It kills the soul of the nation, it robs it of its individuality as a race. It thus renders its political regeneration impossible.

The British rulers of India have only followed the lesson taught by History. They have had considerable experience in the art of conquering other peoples. They have also been conquered by several nations in the early period of their history. They have not exhibited any superhuman sagacity and cunning in thus sapping the foundations of our nationality. All "imperial" races know the trick: it is a device with which all aggressive and vigorous nations, not excepting the Hindus in the days of their glory, have been familiar, Let us see how the "educational" systems of different conquering nations have affected their subjects.

Rome:—The Romans have been the greatest and the wisest "imperial" race on earth. The name of Rome is a synonym for empire. Rome consolidated her empire and attached her subjects to herself by offering them Roman art and culture. The national individuality of the Gaul and the Briton was thus destroyed. No country under Roman dominion ever produced a national literature of its own. The provincial scholars tried to excel in Latin, the language of the ruling race. The grandchildren of the British chiefs who had resisted the Roman invasion of Britain took pride in wearing the toga and speaking the Latin tongue.

The Aryans:—The Hindus were great warriors and conquerors in the days of their youth. They colonized and civilized the whole of India and established their rule over countries which are described as the abode of Vanaras and Rakshasas in the Ramayan. The spread of Hindu dominion over the continent was the work of our great ancestors. They too perpetuated their rule over the subject races by Hinduizing them, by conquering them socially and intellectually. They taught their subjects the Sanskrit language, converted them to the Hindu religion and completely transformed their social life. Nothing of the old "barbarism" remained and the "national" feeling of the tribe also disappeared. Thus did our forefathers consolidated their empire. They were wise men in their generation.

Islam:—The fact that Muhammadan conquerors insisted on a complete revolution in the life of the nations who fell before them is known to all. Persia and Afghanistan lost their old civilizations and were Muhammadanized. India was partially brought under Islamic influence, as we had more resisting power than the Iranians. Akbar laid firm the foundations of the Mogul Empire by teaching us Persian, which gave birth to Urdu. If Urdu had not been invented, how could the descendants of those who fought Babar read the poems composed by Zafar, a representative of his dynasty, with delight and appreciation? The study of Persian literature by some classes of the Hindus was a source of strength to the Muhammadan State. Those Hindus who thus abjured their ancestral speech must have lost something of the fine patriotic feeling that animated the heart of a Brahman, to whom everything associated with Islam was an abomination.

Spain:—Spain has had a large colonial Empire. She left the impress of her civilization on her dependencies. The inhabitants of the Philippines still cherish the Spanish language and the Roman

Catholic faith which they had received from their conquerors. Even to-day Portugal is looked upon as the mother country by colonies who are now politically independent but whose reverence for Camoen, the national poet of Portugal, links them to Portugal with an indissoluble chain.

England & Ireland :—The disastrous effects of the British educational system in countries which have been conquered by the pushing Briton are best illustrated by the havoc it has wrought in Ireland. In India the evil has not gone so deep, as the Hindus possess a strong national individuality and the educational system has found its admirers only among the upper classes as yet. The British Government established schools in Ireland in 1830. They were designed for the purpose of denationalizing the Irish race and thus impairing their power of resisting the foreigner. All the text books except one were prepared by Scotchmen and Englishmen. Irish history and poetry were proscribed. Mr. O'Brien, in the Home Ruler's Manual, informs us that Scott's poem " Breathes there a man with soul so dead " was removed from the text-books to make room for these beautiful lines illustrative of British truthfulness and British poetical genius :—

> " I bless the glory and the grace
> That on my birth have smiled
> And made me in these Christian days,
> A happy English child."

The Irish children were to dishonour their parents and the memory of their ancestors by reciting these lines in the schools. Mr. Sidney Brooks, in his book "New Ireland," is of opinion that the British educational system all but destroyed the Gaelic language, which is now confied to the suburbs but which was universally spoken in Ireland a hundred years ago. The Irish language was ignored, if not actually penalized in the foreign system. The impartial English author bears testimony to ruinous effects of the British educational system in destroying Irish national games and pastimes, music and culture. The national individuality of the race almost perished. The children did not know the history of their nation. They could not acquire a thorough command of the English tongue and they forgot their own language. The thread of historic continuity was suddenly snapped in these hybrid outcastes who were divorced from their own civilization and could not assimilate another. And with the decay of their language and institutions, "the true fibre of Irish manhood began to rot away." Moral and intellectual stagnation set in. A mob of slaves without a memory of their past was the product of their educational system which found the Irish people with a national civilization and left them without one. Thus the Irish acquired a little "knowledge" at the cost of their national life. They sacrificed. the end for the means.

Now, after a century of painful experience, the Irish have been awakened to a sense of their miserable position. They have formed the Gaelic League to revive the old language and music, the old games and customs.

America & Cuba :—To come to the history of our own times, America is trying her best to Americanize her new subjets in Asia and Australia. Persons who crave free and compulsory education as a boon from the Government should take note of the fact that the Americans granted this "concession" to the Cubans and the Hawailans of their own free will immediately after the conquest. The American Government even supplies the text-books free of charge in Cuba! Thus these islanders are being civilized away. A letter from the Director of Education in Porto Rice to the supervisors of English education contained the following injunction:—

" Supervising the teaching of English in Porto Rico, which you now undertake, is *one of the most important duties of the hour.*"

It is stated in the Report of the Commissioner of Education, U. S. A., that the want of a knowledge of English was the greatest difficulty in the way of those who wished to become American in thought, culture and loyalty.

Germany and Poland:—At present a conflict is raging between the German authorities and their Polish subjects on this vital question of education.

The Poles are keen on preserving their language, which is almost the sole remaining symbol of their national unity. The Germans desire to get rid of a discordant element in the body politic by Germanising the Poles—a process to which the latter sturdily refuse to submit. The struggle between the two nations has not ended. The Poles refuse to send their children to German schools. Thus do subject races resist the attempts of their conquerors to denationalize them.

THE EFFECTS OF THE BRITISH EDUCATIONAL SYSTEM

We have shown that the British rulers of India established schools and colleges in order to consolidate their Empire and weaken our Hindu institutions and polity. We have also pointed out that in doing so they only followed the example of great conquerors all the world over. Let us now discuss the actual effects of the British educational system on our character and institutions.

The strength of a nation consists in the vitality of its permanent and distinctive institutions and on its moral calibre. The two questions which every student of sociology need ask about a people are: What sort of *men* are they? Are they brave truthful, self-respecting? And then, what sort of institutions do they possess? Are they calculated to further their progress? Are they loved and cherished by the people?

If it can be proved that an educational system weakens our national institutions and lowers our character, as a race, that system stands self-condemned. We need not waste breath in discussing its merits and demerits.

I. *National Institutions.* National institutions are the sign and symbol of national individuality. All men have the organs of sense; the intellect, affections, feelings, passions, love and hate, jealousy and sympathy, avarice and philanthropy are common to all civilized people. All men eat and drink, wear clothes and talk to each other, take part in the religious worship of some sort or other, and pay homage to some historical past. The essence of national life consists in the particular religion which we follow, the particular history which we cherish, the particular language that we love and speak, the particular social life which we appreciate. Language, social life, religion, literature, history—these form the living forces in a community which mould national character and aspirations. It is for their protection and preservation that we create the State, the army, the navy and the police. It is for the defence of these beloved institutions, the heirlooms which we have inherited from our ancestors, that we desire to attain Swaraj. It is for these sacred treasures that every nation sacrifices ease and wealth and life from generation to generation. They form the nerves and fibres of the organism called the State. They constitute the foundations of the National Polity. The nation decays when we cease to love them with a passionate all-absorbing love.

National institutions are thus the essential marks of national life. There can be no Nation without national institutions. It is mere moonshine to talk of 'nationality' when there are no living institutions corresponding to the idea of nationality. Nationality is kept alive and strengthened by real institutions which are a part and parcel of our daily life which we have been taught to love and revere from childhood. It is not fed on speeches, aspirations, arguments, imagination, cosmopolitanism and such like in substantial stuff. An exposition of Bluntschli's theory of nationality will not infuse into him a keen feeling of nationality, If his daily life teaches him to despise, or neglect national institutions, he can never be patriotic. Experience is a more efficient teacher than words and logic.

Now let us see how the British educational system de-Hinduizes us and causes the decay of our national institutions, thereby hindering the growth of the feeling of Hindu Unity and national life.

(i) *Language.*—Language is a most important national institution. It is often *the* distinguishing feature of nationality. A Dutch proverb says, No language, no nationality. Language is the bond of society. It marks off our countrymen from the stranger. Bhasha is also the mother, as the Ganga is the Mother, for without Bhasha we cannot live even for a day.

Language not only unites the men of the present generation and enables them to deliberate together on national affairs, but it also enables us to hold communion with the dead. *It is the key to national history.* The words and deeds of our forefathers are enshrined in our language,—in Sanskrit, Hindi and Panjabi—like pearl in a shell. National language thus preserves historical continuity, which is the life of the nation. A common historical background is one of the indispensable conditions of national growth. Common political ideals and aspirations are impossible without a common past.

Language is also the guardian of the national literature, which voices the national spirit. A nation's literature is one of its most precious possessions. Carlyle has written that if he were asked to give up the Indian Empire or Shakespear, he would gladly forego the former, but not the great national poet of England. The Empire, he says, must go some day, but Shakespear represents the eternal, im perishable wealth of England.

It is language then that preserves and interprets National History and Literature. It stands sentinal at the gate of the National Temple and no one who does not answer its call "Who goes there" can enter the sacred precincts.

The effect of the British educational system on the National Language is disastrous.

The Hindu nation has two languages which it should teach to every member of the race. One is an imperial language: the other is the provincial tongue.

Corresponding to the double consciousness of tribal and of national unity, we have two languages for every cultivated Hindu who wishes to discharge his duty towards his country. There is the Sanskrit, the language of Empire and Religion, the imperial and sacred language of the Hindus; and then comes the Vernacular, the tribal tongue of different provinces, Hindi, Bengali Marathi, etc. When a Hindu addresses the whole nation he uses Sanskrit: when he confines himself to his own particular province, he employs his vernacular. Sanskrit embodies the common imperial past of the nation.

How does the British educational system affect our languages, Sanskrit and Hindi or Marathi or Gujrati? One fact will enable us to realize the situation better than a whole page of exposition.

I, an educated Hindu, am writing an article in English in this paper and communicate my thought not to Englishmen or Americans but to my own friends and countrymen, living in the same province and the same country and speaking the same language as myself.

The series of articles is the most conclusive proof of the disastrous effects of this educational system on our languages.

If I had followed nature, if our whole life had not been rendered ridiculous, artificial and miserable by this educational system, I should have written in Sanskrit to appeal to my countrymen in Bengal,

Bombay or Madras (an aspiration which has not altogether been abandoned) and in Hindi to address the people of my province,

I take this occasion to apologize to the Ancestors and to my countrymen of the present generation for thus dishonouring and weakening a national institution. My only excuse is that the pernicious habit of reading newspapers and magazines published in English which prevails among our upper classes compels me to address them through the medium of the language of a foreign country situated 7,000 miles away from Lahore. The upper classes are the brain of the nation. If we wish to rescue a man from a bog we have to enter it ourselves and give him a helping hand. It is for this reason that I stoop to compromise my national dignity by indulging in this artificial and ludicrous practice.

(ii) *History.*—National History is the *sine qua non* of national unity and growth. A nation that has no past must lack cohesion and patriotism. Common hero-worship is the bond of society.

The British rulers of India teach our boys what is really a caricature of Hindu history. The text-books written by the Lethbridges and Hunters of the Anglo-Indian community give us no idea of our ancient greatness. They impress on the minds of our boys the notion that we have been an incapable race since the dawn of history and that our only function has been to lose battles one after another in the course of centuries. There is no mention of all that should be the pride of every Hindu.

Woe to the nation that allows its children to read history as it is written by its foreign conquerors! No people with a particle of self-respect would tolerate it even for a moment. We may be unable to emulate our ancestors: but let us at least refrain from reviling them.

A man who sends his son to an Anglo-Indian school commits the sin of *pitri-ninda,* the vilification of national heroes, the dishonouring of national history.

(iii) *Literature*:—Language and literature go together. Sanskrit literature must lose ground before English if the present system endures. Our boys have to study Scott and Milton, while they are utterly ignorant of Sanskrit literature, which is equally inspiring and artistic. English is already taking the place of Sanskrit as the medium of communication among Hindus belonging to different provinces. English is a compulsory subject for all classes at school and college. The Hindu nation must choose between Sanskrit and English. Under the present system Sanskrit literature and learning will gradually perish and with its decay will fall the whole edifice of Hindu civilization. For our society draws its morality and religion, its social spirit and its laws, from the Shastras. The decline of Sanskrit learning will reduce us to the condition of a disorganized mob without national institutions.

Ayurveda is being undermined by Government Medical Colleges. A Hindu youngman can become a "graduate" in Philosophy without reading anything of Hindu metaphysics - the highest product of Hindu genius! Religion is proscribed in Government schools. The study of the Upanishads and the Smrities is no part of the University curriculum.

The British education system will destroy Sanskrit literature and learning which is the pride and glory of our race and the well-spring of our moral and social ideals.

This unnatural system will also kill out our vernaculars. Already we see the sorrowful spectacle of parents writing letters to their children in English, of people reading newspapers in English, of students giving English name to their clubs and associations, of national assemblies possessing English names! There are thousands of Hindus in Oudh who have received "èducation" at Anglo-Indian schools, and can not therefore read the Ramayan with facility. The language of the people is systematically ignored in the University curriculum. It is the case of Ireland over again. Instead of teaching the boys through medium of their own language, the Anglo-Indians compel them to answer examination papers in history and geography in English! I wonder if Englisb boys at Eton learn history from text-books written in Chinese. With literature will go our culture and art. Indeed, the decay of Hindu intellectual life is patent to all who have eyes to see. Sir George Birdwood makes the following candid confession: "We are destroying their faith and their literature and their arts, and the continuity of the spontaneous development of their civilization and their great historical personality; in a word, we are destroying the very soul of the nation."

(iv) *Social Life.*—Social life is a national institution. It grows and changes like all other institutions. But it is all times a determining factor in national life. It is the product of the instinct which leads all nations to adapt themselves to their surroundings. It creates the environments in the midst of which it is possible for national intellect and morals to grow and develop. A natural healthy social life, suited to the time and place, is a national asset of the greatest value.

Social life is also a mark and symbol of national unity. It should not be tampered with in an irreverent spirit.

The British educational system throws our social life out of gear. It upsets all rules and conventions and weakens our sense of social duty. It leads to indescribable confusion in dress, modes of speech and rules of etiquettc. The climax is reached in such instances as that of the man who said, on entering a temple, "Good evening, Vishnu!". Many young Hindu take to shaving their moustache even when they are not in mourning for the loss of their parents. Others might insist on being buried after death. A few have married European wives without converting them to Hinduism. The national social life is thus thrown off its hinges. The Muhammadans gave at the first shock from which it has not been able to recover. The present educational system tends to disorganize and destroy it altogether.

Thus the "Educational" system established by Anglo-Indians saps the vitality of national institutions, which are the source of national feeling and aspiration.

(v) *Character.*—What idea does not the British educational system represent? And what ideal does it inculcate? If it does not stand for any great idea and does not touch a great ideal, it must have a ruinous effect on Hindu character. Ideas and ideals quicken the moral life of a people. The only idea which it may be said to represent is the acquisition of a knowledge of the language: the only ideal that it seems to place before us is that of becoming a graduate,

Idealism.—the soul of an individual's moral life, has no place in this system, for it deliberately excludes religion from its curriculum. And it does not teach national history either. Religion and patriotism are the two great forces which have made men great in different countries and ages. An educational system which does not value either of them must produce men without an ideal and without backbone!

Hence the students of our colleges have no faith in anything—religion or politics or art or science. They believe only in things of the world. Those among them who have risen above materialism or moral inertia have come under the influence of powerful forces originating outside the Anglo-Indian educational system. The majority of our graduates have lost the fine old faith of their fathers in Hindu social institutions and have not found any other moral basis of life. The Truth that was does not appeal to them: and they have not caught a glimpse of the Truth that shall be. And where there is no vision the people perisheth.

Patriotism:—must decay under a system which discourages the study of our national past. British 'educational' policy alienates the cultured classes from the common people, diminishes their reverence and love for great heroes like Rama, Krishna and Guru Govind, and curbs their political aspirations. Mr. Gokhale tells us that Mr. Ranade wrote an essay depreciating the British system of Government in comparison with Mahratta rule, "Sir Alexander Grant, who was then Principal of Elphinstone College, and who had great admiration for Mr. Ranade's talents, sent for him and after pointing out to him the error of his views, said to him: 'Youngman, you should not thus run down a Government which is educating you and doing so much for your people.' And to mark his serious displeasure he suspended Mr. Ranade's scholarship for six months." The Government has turned its colleges into comfortable prisons for our youngmen, who are prevented from reading nationalist newspapers and attending meetings at which sound political ideas are promulgated. Woe to those who lose their birthright of learning about the condition of their country and honouring the greatmen of the nation for a mess of pottage in the shape of a license for practice at the Bar or a Government diploma of graduation! They sacrifice the end for the means: they lose the substance and run after the shadow. They demoralise themselves and teach others to do violence to their conscience. Thus the British educational system promotes servility, cowardice and social decay. Sir W. Lee Warner, in his little book "The Citizen of India", teaches our boys the following precious truth:

"There is no 'drain' of wealth from India to England. The former rulers of India never cared for their people.

India is growing in prosperity under British rule."

Men who send their sons to School where such

books are taught injure the nation and betray their trust as guardians of their children.

Courage is not a quality which can grow in the unhealthy moral atmosphere of our colleges. Students who have to show respect to officials for whom they have really no love in their hearts, cannot possess any moral courage. A life of Fraud and Falsehood can never build up character. The strain which the artificial method of teaching through the medium of English puts on our energies undermines our physical stamina and exhausts out vitality even before we enter on the struggle of life.

As to the minor virtues which have adorned Hindu character from time immemorial, simplicity, temperance, courtesy, family affection, and respect for elders, the British 'educational' system is notoriously fatal to their development.

Patriotism and spirituality—the two great character—making forces—are absent from this "educational" system. The smaller virtues which are also inherited by Hindus, decay through the influence of ill-digested European ideas and the example of third-rate European professors.

The Hindu character is ruined. The springs of the national moral life are poisoned. If a man gain the world, but lose his own soul, what shall it profit him? So said a teacher of old. And if a nation should acquire the learning of the whole world but lose its life, its institutions and its character, how will it survive? We cannot give our life in exchange for a smattering of English literature and Science. We cannot consent to part with our nationhood for such paltry advantages.

The British Educational System is the present of two great evils—Denationalization and demoralization. It weakens Hindu social and religious institutions and it undermines patriotism and moral courage. No device could be more effectual for accelerating our decline as a nation.

There are several other consequences of the establishment of Government schools and colleges which deserve notice:—

(a) *The Social Degradation of the Hindu race*:—The Briton, having acquired the power and glory which belonged to the Kshatriya, tries to step into the place held by the Brahman in order that he may complete the *social* conquest of India by England. Political and Military predominance must be supported by social supremacy, otherwise it can not endure. A nation, which has only lost its national State, is not crushed, it is under a merely temporary eclipse, But if it should gradually lose the sense of self-respect and national individuality by mixing with foreigners *on terms of inequality*, it can not rise again. *Political subjection is not so grave an evil as social serfdom to Europeans.*

Schools and colleges convert our Brahmans,

Kshatriyas and Vaisyas into docile and respectful pupils of Christians and Anglo-Indian officials. The conquerors get an opportunity of posing as teachers and benefactors of the "subject" race. Our boys learn to occupy a position of social inferiority to Europeans in everyday life, for the teacher must always sit above the pupil. They begin to look up to members of the conquering race as their moral and spiritual guides. Thus does Brahmanhood too pass from the Hindu Brahman to the Englishman. Another victory in the conflict of civilization is won by the Briton. The Brahman who should teach our children, is displaced by the pushing foreigner. The social conquest proceeds apace, killing out national pride and self-respect and the feeling of national identity along our upper and middle classes.

All "low-abiding" subjects of thc British Empire are required to pay taxes and obey the laws established by the Government. No man is compelled to do more for the bureaucray. How mean and unpatriotic must those people be, who voluntarily accept the discipleship of the bureaucracy and become not only subjects but also pupils and social inferiors to Anglo-Indiadom.

(b) *The prestige of the bureaucracy* :—The Government of India should control and guide all activities in Hindu society, if it wishes to enhance its prestige and take the place of an earthly Providence in the mind of the people. The educational system adds to the prestige of the officials who manage it. They stand forth before the public as instructors and receive spontaneous homage from unthinking men who do not understand their policy. A Government school in a village impresses on the imagination of the people great truth that the Sirkar is an all-powerful, all-absorbing, omni present and omnicient agency controlled by men of wonderful power and wisdom. The Sirkar is a very Ishwara on earth: it is here, there and every where: it does so many things and does them well. Verily, saith the rustic philosopher, the Sirkar is the only reality in the world: all else is *maya*. It has no hands, but it works; it has no eyes but it sees. The Sirkar is the source of all Life.

(c) *The Loss of Self-Government.*—A subject people should at least try to keep the direction of their social affairs in their own hands as far as possible. All interference on the part of foreigners, even if it is well-meant, should be nipped in the bud. The political and military activities of the nation must pass under the control of foreigners as a necessary consequence of subjugation. But we need not give them all when they ask only an inch. Those who send their sons to Anglo-Indian schools are following the stupid policy of surrendering to Government more than it demands of us as a conquering power: Education, Religion and Social customs should form the sacred circle within which all unhallowed foreign control is inadmissible. The British Government does not compel us to resort to its schools. Why should we give up the duty of managing our own affairs in these spheres of national life and activity which are still under our own control. The British Educational system will destroy Kashi, Nuddea, and other centres of Hindu learning. *It robs us of our capacity for self-government in educational matters.* The old-world Pundit who opens an "indigenous" school on his own account practises self-government on a small scale. But enlightened public men who patronize Government Colleges, help the extension of bureaucratic influence in our social life. Cursed be those who destroy the small remnants of self-government which a jealous and grasping bureaucracy still allows to a subject people. We have lost much: we have fallen. Why should we lose more and fall lower? Why should we give up the privilege of self-government in Educational affairs?

It should be clearly understood that all extension of Government control and supervision involves a corresponding decay in the vitality of the people. Everything that is done by the bureaucracy must take something out of the hands of the people. Government control and initiative must be fatal to the growth of the capacity for self-government among the nation. This is self-evident. Light must recede as the shadows advance. Even a beneficial institution established by Government impairs our power of establishing and managing it through our own energy and enterprise. The loss of self-government, even if accompanied with a temporary advantage, is to be dreaded like a calamity, for it saps the moral qualities which are necessary for complete self-government and which it should be our duty to foster. When it brings in its train other evils, it is of course an unmitigated curse. A public library established by Government only hinders the growth of popular civic life while it confers a temporary benefit on us. Even a *pathshala* or a temple which is established by Government for the promotion of Sanskrit learning is injurious to our national interests for it undermines the habits of self-help and self-reliance, which alone can save the Hindu race and its religion. But Government schools and colleges rob us of all that we hold dear—self-respect, character, patriotism, national literature and history, and finally self-Government in educational affairs.

(d) The Extension of British Influence in Indian States.—The Universities have been efficient instruments for driving the thin end of the wedge of British influence into the affairs of Indian States. It is no where provided in any treaty that a ruling Indian Prince should connect the schools and colleges of his State with the British Univer-

sities. Yet we are so foolish that we cut at the root of our own national life by sending up our boys in the States for University Examinations. The Government is not to blame in this respect. It does not compel any Raja or Nawab to place his educational department in partial subordination to the British Educational Service. Our incapable and indolent Ministers have of their own free will compromised the dignity of our States and impaired their vitality by allowing and even asking the British Universities to extend their operations in their territory. Is it impossible for states which collect their own revenues and administer their internal affairs in all departments, to establish their own schools and colleges under the sole authority and guidance of the Head of the State? As I observe the humilitating spectacle of an Indian State requesting British Universities to exercise control and authority in their Colleges, I am reminded of Raja Sir T. Madhav Rao's pregnant words:—

"The longer I live, observe and think, the more deeply do I feel that there is no community on the face of the earth which suffers . . . . . more from self-invited, self-accepted or self-aggravated, and therefore avoidable evils than the Hindu community."

(I am quoting from memory).

(e) *The Industrial Backwardness of the Nation*:—The British educational system serves to

f

convert the sons of our bankers, traders and landowners into dependents of the bureaucracy while the field of industrial and commercial enterprise is left open for the European settlers in India. The University curriculum prepares our youngmen for no useful profession. It encourages literary culture but proscribes commercial training and technical studies. Mr. Chesney has recognized this defect of the British educational system in his book on "The Indian Polity", The inevitable effect of that system is the creation of an ever-increasing class of useless persons, who know no art or trade and who are compelled to serve the administration as officials or lawyers in order to earn a living. The foundations of our economic life are thus undermined. It is sad, indescribably sad, to see sons of shop-keepers and bankers trying to "rise" in the social scale by taking to the profession of a lawyer. They suffer from a strange perversion of judgment. They imagine that a lawyer or an official is entitled to greater social esteem than an honest shopkeeper or landowner. The educational system tends to incapacitate our youths for a commercial or industrial career. It smooths the path of the European exploiter before him. It will turn the children of our Vaishyas into hangers-on the bureaucracy, lawyers and officials while European capitalists are getting our trade and industry more and more into their hands. The process of dethroning the Vaishya from his pedestal of financial power and installing the European planter or merchant or banker in his place is in progress. And the Universities help materially in the process. They facilitate and accelerate the economic enslavement of our race.

SANSKRIT VERSUS ENGLISH

Having shown the numerous evils that flow from the unnatural and artificial educational system which the British have established in India, I now proceed to expose certain fallacies which are current among many "educated" people with regard to its effects on our character and progress. It is wonderful that we Indians accept wrong ideas and ideals without a word of protest. We are lacking in the critical faculty. With regard to the educational problem, we have been living in a sort of fool's paradise, hugging the chains that have bound us. It is time that we should clear our minds of *cant*.

It is a favourite notion with many patriots that this system with its insistence on English literature as a compulsory subject of tuition, provides us with an instrument of communication between the different Indian people which are divided by differences of language. This system is supposed to have conferred a common language, the *sina qua non* of the Indian unity, on our people. With its progress, therefore, the cause of Indian Nationalism is bound up in a definite manner. The English language is regarded as the future *lingua franca* of India. Thus it is imagined that the conquest has conferred this inestimable boon on us.

This India is most pernicious. It implies an absurdity. It contradicts the teachings of history and sociology. It is derived from a superficial study of post-Mutiny Indian politics. It is a product of the minds of ill-informed students of sociology devoid of insight into Reality.

If English is to be the language of unified India, then it appears that a united India means a denationalized India. The great semi-independent States like Nepal, Udaipur and Hyderabad cannot boast of a denationalised and demoralised class of "Graduates" such as are turned out by British Universities, in India. They still cherish the national language and need not forget it to make English the language of public business. The states are under no necessity of sacrificing Indian culture and civilization. They are and ought to be the bulwarks of the national civilization against the attacks of alien ideals. Hence those politicians who set up English as the language of United India confine their attention to "British" India that portion of our country which has been completely subjugated by foreigners. They do not think of those Indians who still enjoy some of the elementary rights of humanity, of which we who live in British

India have been deprived. It would be a curious plan of union which should omit to consider the people of the States which enjoy a large measure of self-governmet.

Then, again, the principle which insists on the adoption of the conqueror's language for our national purposes is radically unsound. It is destructive of national solidarity. It may, under certain circumstances, cut at the root of our national existence altogether. It is an accident that the great majority of Indians have fallen under the dominion of one European power. The fact conceals from us the dangerous nature of the programme which would base unity on a foreign language. There are some Indians who are subjects of the French Republic. Others own allegiance to Portugal. What shall we do with these fellowmen of ours? Shall we shun them altogether simply because they are not "British" subjects? Are they comprehenced in our plan of union? Those Politicians who adopt English as the *lingua franca* of India evidently believe that Indians who have not been conquered by Britain have no part or lot with us. They see only the red colour on the map of India. If India were to be partitioned among different European powers a contingency which did not appear impossible in the eighteenth century, the Anglicised politicians would call several Congresses transacting business in various European languages. For, according to them, the language of the conquering race provides the principle of Unity in this chaotic mass of languages and dialects. The plan would be fatal to the very existence of the Hindu nation.

This consideration brings me to the great truth which I wish to emphasize. *The principle of Unity exists* WITHIN *a community and cannot be imported from* WITHOUT. All uniformity produced by the adoption of external devices is deceptive. It will not lead to unity, as will lack the quickening soul which keeps an institution alive. If all Indians were to speak Esperanto which is a much easier language to learn than English that would not stimulate national feeling or preserve national institutions.

Let us not be deceived by the glamour of the present or base our national movement on the errors of a purblind generation. Decades are as moments in the history of a nation. The illusion of Anglicisation, from which we have been suffering for the last thirty years, must be destroyed. The Brahma of National Self-Realization is hidden from us where this Maya prevails. Sanskrit is the only national tongue for all India—the language of our noble religion and the tongue associated with India's highest hopes and happiness. It is the medium of inter-communication among the various States, and it is the language of science and scholarship. It speaks to us of our common past and can furnish the only solid foundation for a genuine national movement. Why should I seek proficiency in English if I do not want to be a lawyer or a servant of the British Government? A tolerable knowledge of that language, or even French or German, would give me access to stores of modern civilization. But I must learn Sanskrit well in order to join the ranks of the educated classes in India. No Hindu who is ignorant of Sanskrit can have any pretensions to culture.

But some people say that Sanskrit is a dead language, and that it cannot be commonly used for purpose of national business. This idea is altogether erroneous. It is easier for a Hindu to learn Sanskrit than English. Sanskrit is not dead—it is we who are dead. Of course, we cannot deliver lectures before the British public in Sanskrit. We cannot write articles to advise and inform the Bureaucracy in Sanskrit. But those who wish to teach the people and build up a nation, must part company with those who traffic in unreal political charlatanism. Those who desire to make a great and united Nation must take their stand on Sanskrit as the eternal refuge and glory of the Indian people.

We have got into the habit of writing and speaking in English on public affairs. There is really no reason why a graduate who knows both Sanskrit and English should not use the former where he now employs the latter. Sanskrit will come to him more naturally than English. But it is a fatality pursuing all conquered races that they dig their own graves. The Hindus of Northern India voluntarily gave up Sanskrit and took to Persian under the Mogul regime, and a similar suicidal policy is being pursued at present on a vaster scale.

THE SO-CALLED AWAKENING

There is another error which has found acceptance in all circles and which is, if possible, even more grotesque and disastrous. The idea is abroad that the British educational system is the parent of Progress. It is supposed to have conferred on us poor benighted Asiatics the great notions of liberty, political enfranchisement, social advancement, and what not. It is said to have vevified our decaying civilization and rescued us from the slough of despondency into which we had fallen. It is the mother of "New India". Shall we kill the hen that lays the golden eggs ?

The advocates of the British educational system assume too much. They have to prove that a system which teaches no religious ideals and discourages patriotism can confer any benefits on a people. They must show that the English-educated classes have brought about any political awakening I think that our political aspirations have been curbed and crushed by this system. The ideal of co-operation with the bureaucracy—which means playing second fiddle only—as the *summum bonum* of Indian humanity, could be evolved only out of the dwarfed imagination of half-educated men who could not think clearly and boldly. The tree is judged by its fruits. The vast majority of those who have been educated at schools and colleges are continually engaged in undermining the foundations of their nationality. They serve as assistants to the bureaucracy, as teachers in Government schools, as lawyers and barristers in British courts of law, and thus enhance the power and prestige of the bureaucratic rulers of the country. They are helping in the destruction of the national genius for original and independent pursuits. That is what the "English-educated" class is doing—it is dragging the nation to a lower level in the scale of humanity by accepting the ideals, the discipleship, and the patronage of the bureaucracy. It has been truly said that if there were not a poor and ignorant peasantry on one side and a degenerate and unpatriotic "educated" class on the other, things in India would be different from what they are at present.

A few men here and there have escaped the soul-corroding, denationalizing influence of this educational system chiefly through the agency of various religious movements which, of course, can not owe their origin to British schools and colleges. These few men have not learnt the lessons of sacrifice and spirituality, moral courage and patriotism, at the feet of Anglo-Indian officials who teach in the Colleges. For of thorns men do not gather figs. The innate vitality of Indian civilisation is not yet exhausted, otherwise there would be no hope for us. That civilisation has given us the few great men we have produced in the 19th century—Ranjit Singh, Dayanand, Ram Krishna, Salar Jang, Vivekanand and a few others. How can the soulless instruction given in the Anglo-Indian schools produce great men? The effects of Anglo-Indian education were seen in the first generation of Bengalis who were turned out from Government Colleges—a set of fashionable, denationalized, unpatriotic, selfish creatures, the very scum of Indian humanity thrown up to the surface by official patronage. Scores were converted to Christianity. Since then the old Hindu civilization has asserted itself against the baneful effects of this system, and the evil has been to some extent counteracted. But we must devise a thorough cure for this malady. It has been asserted that the ideas of "liberty" and "nationality" have been conferred on us by this Anglo-Indian system. These ideas are said to be peculiarly Western products, and the study of Mill and Thomas Paine is supposed to have fired our hearts with a passion for freedom. Mr. S. Nair, who is now a Government servant, cried: "You cannot urge a man into slavery in the English language." Mr. Gokhale is of opinion that the "new spirit" has been produced by the education imparted at Government schools and colleges.

It would be strange, passing strange, if such ideas as those of liberty and nationality could grow in the servile and denationalizing atmosphere of Government colleges. And how has Afghanistan got such a firm hold on these great ideas? How have the Gurkhas acquired their intense love of liberty? Our "educated" men have learned a few quotations from Burke and Mill; they have read sonnets in praise of Liberty. But of the real thing, patriotism, many of them know as little as the man in the moon. Why, a man who possessed European ideas of patriotism and national self-respect would never send his sons to schools that lead to denationalization. And some of us serve the bureaucracy and then prate of "national" unity! Parrots repeat Vedic Mantras and the holy name of liberty is dessecrated in the mouths of men who talk glibly of patriotism while helping the bureaucratic regime as lawyers and officials! As for our "Congressmen", they seem to have lost the primary instincts of self-respecting nations. They think they have learned the lesson of patriotism" at British schools and colleges. Queer "patriotism" indeed which makes its votarics regard it glory to occupy a position of permanent inferiority playing the second fiddle again-to Englishmen in the "constitution of the Government!

The Fallacy of The "Awakening".—The Indian National Congress is often supposed to be the outcome of the British educational system. And it is taken for granted that the Congress is a monument of wisdom and patriotism. It follows therefore that the political progress of India depends on the British educational system.

Is the Congress a sign of political progress or of decay? Does it represent an advance in political ideas and methods, or does it imply a retrogression in the political life of the nation? This point must be settled before we can pronounce on the merits and decmerits of the British educational system, as it is believed in some circles that the Anglo-Indian colleges have led to a great political awakening, which is symbolized by the Congress. This erroneous idea has not been got rid of even by some Nationalists.

If the Congress were the quintessence of the Indian Nation's wisdom and patriotism, I should be very doubtful as to the future of that nation. *The Congress marks a retrograde step in the political* life of India, and the British educational system is responsible for the decline in India's political morality and sagacity which made the Congress possible. For such an assembly could not exist in a country where natural feelings of self-respect and pride had not been undermined by some cause or other. Why could there be no Congress in the year 1820 or

1860 ? Let us reflect on this question. The year 1884, in which the Congress was founded marks the period when Indian intelligence and national feeling fell prostrate before the systematic assaults of Anglo-Indians, and the people ceased to hope for any serious improvement in their political status and condition.

Let us analyse the idea for which the Congress stands or stood. The ideal of association with the bureaucracy which has been proclaimed by the Congress in the resolutions, and the agitation in favour of simultaneous examinations and the admission of Indians to high offices in the service of the British Government, clearly represent a sad decay of national self-respect and of the ethical standard of the nation.

Let us not be misled by appearances. We some times deceive ourselves that we are more civilized than our grand-fathers because we hold so many meetings, deliver speeches in the right Royal London style, and possess newspapers and journals. But *noise is not life.* We know the proverb which says that empty vessels make much noise. Maharashtra boasts of many newspapers, dailies and weeklies, while Nepal and Afghanistan do not enjoy the luxury of newspaper reading. But which has more true and vigorous national life Maharashtra or, Afghanistan ? Some of us have learned all the beauties of the theory of nationality, but are the Gurkhas politically in a worse condition than the Bengalis simply because they cannot discourse on the blessings of liberty? We must penetrate through the shows of things to the reality. We have to find out if our *views* and *methods* are superior to those which the "uneducated" people of the early nineteenth century appreciated and advocated for the political progress of the country.

As to the methods of political work, the majority of the English-educated classes shrink from self-help and national self-assertion. They believe in oratory and pursuation. They have preached for twenty years and more that the only method of political advancement is the use of the tongue and the pen to the exclusion of other instruments. They have degenerated into mere poltroons and windbags, and want to impose their wrong ideas on the sturdy peasants who know that politics is not a war of words between bureaucrats and their courtly disciples. They know the essential principles of politics and are not deluded into erroneous opinions like the English-educated wiseacres who deliver eloquent speeches before the English tailors and cobblers and grocers. The idea of "agitation" for political purposes was altogether unknown to our ancestors who lived before the era of schools and colleges, for they never suspected that a disarmed nation could work out its salvation by the use of its tongue and lungs. They did not imagine that vast gatherings of cowardly serfs, even if held everyday would induce Government to relinquish any of its powers and privileges. They never made any mistakes on fundamental questions like the nature of British rule, the character and aims of the British people, the need of maintaining social and political isolation from the rulers, the futility of mere words in political matters and the future destiny of India. On all these points, their ideas were sound and natural. But strange and absurd opinions have been manufactured in Government colleges under the guidance of clever Anglo-Indians and are now held up to our admiration as tokens of a great "political awakening," as symbols of a " new spirit " of which Messrs Surendranath Bannerjee, Ranade, Mehta, W. C. Bonnerji and others are the apostles. These men were the " enlightened ones," the leaders who dispelled the " darkness " in which brave old-fashioned peasants and Rajas wandered blindly about, and who inaugurated the era of "light and progress". Let us examine what the "awakening" was like. What were the antecedents of the "leaders" who had emerged from the colleges with the new gospel of political puerility and emasculation, which was to be preached from the platform of that small body with a big name 'The Indian National Congress".

Mr. Surrendra Nath Banerji, the orator of the " awakening," established a college for which he could not find the name of any Indian hero, and so had to fix on Ripon. He praises Alexander Duff, the Christian missionary, in terms of warm appreciation. Then again he pleaded for simultaneous examinations, which should enable more Indians to ruin their county by joining an aristocratic service which holds itself aloof from the masses. Mr. Ranade was thrice invited to accept the honour and dignity of the Dewan of large Hindu States, but his denationalized proclivities led him to cling to his post under the British Government, This was the "new spirit", which taught Hindu scholars to prefer subordinate places under the British to honour and power under a Hindu Raja in a free State. Mr. Mehta is so great a friend of India that he called the British educational system "a great boon," while at the same time he was convinced that this system would clear the way for Christianity." (Mehta's Speeches—Ed. by Chintamani). He was the man who uttered that blasphemous sentence which makes every Hindu burn with shame:—

"Lord Ripon, Lord Buddha styled on earth".

This champion of the "awakening" compared a Christian Viceroy to, a Hindu *avatar*, one of the greatest men, if not the greatest man indeed, that the world has yet produced. He also declared that "his faith was large even in Anglo-Indians". And, last but not least, we have Mr. Gokhale one of those patriots who could not choose a better name for the college which was supported by their noble self-sacrifice than that of an English Governor of Bombay.

So much for the apostles of this "new" dispensation which has been the product of British schools and colleges and which postulates *permanent subordination and inferiority to Englishmen as its ideal.*

We need not study history to find out that the "education" imparted in Government schools and colleges has blinded us to the Primary truths of political science which were clear as day light to those noblemen and peasants who had not come under Anglo-Indian influence. We may look around us to-day and discover that the "uneducated" unsophisticated people still possess sound ideas on important questions like the essential nature of British Rule and the methods of political work. The artisans of the towns and the peasants in the villages look upon the British as a strange people who will not mix with them and with whom they should not mix. In their hearts they are convinced of the superiority of their fine old civilisation. They have shown their political capacity and insight on many occasions, . The repeal of plague regulations, the prohibition of the sale of beef in a manner which offended the religious susceptabilities of the Hindus, belief for the indebtedness of the Deccan ryots—these and other necessary reforms have not been obtained through the efforts of the orators and politicians of the Congress school but havebeen due to the spontaneous united action of the masses of the people. Had the common people sat at the feet of the Congress "leaders", they would never have succeeded in remedying the evils from which they suffered.

Thus recent history also proves that the illiterate peasants and townsmen have more commonsense and insight than the English-educated graduates who have preached the gospel of the so-called "awakening". The people know how to help themselves, whatever the misguided platform speakers may say.

The much-talked-of political "awakening" which has been traced to the education given in Government Schools is a myth and a deluslon, This blessed educational system has given birth to the class of political buffoons mimics who expose us to the ridicule of the world by preaching the association with the bureaucracy in the administration is the panacca of all our social and political ills, and that a fallen nation does not need self-help, self-respect, and the power to stand on its own legs for its political regeneration.